Revise BTEC National Sport Revision Guide
ISBN 9781292150482
IMPORTANT ASSESSMENT UPDATE

As a result of feedback from the Department for Education, there have been some updates to the Set Task for **Unit 2 for BTEC Nationals in Sport**.

These updates mean there are now some changes required to this book, which are listed below. You need to be aware of these when using this book for revision.

Changes to assessment of Unit 2: Fitness Training and Programming for Health, Sport and Well-being	Changes to Unit 2 Revision Guide	
Part A will be issued **1 week** ahead of Part B (instead of 2 weeks).	**About your Unit 2 assessment**	p84
	It is noted that Part A is issued 2 weeks before Part B. **Part A will now be issued 1 week before Part B**	
You have **4 hours** to complete Part A (instead of 8 hours).	It is noted that you have 8 hours to complete Part A. **You now have 4 hours to complete Part A.**	
Part B must be completed in **2 hours and 30 minutes** (instead of 2 hours).	It is noted that you have 2 hours to complete Part B. **You will now complete Part B in 2 hours and 30 minutes.**	
Details on notes prepared in Part A that can be taken into Part B You will be expected to do preparatory work in Part A and can take up to four sides of A4 notes into the Part B supervised assessment. Your notes: • are in response to the information provided in the scenario in the **Part A** set task information • must contain **bullets** and **not** extended answers • can be hand-written or typed.	It is stated that in Part A you will conduct independent research and produce 4 sides of A4 notes to use in Part B. **Your 4 sides of A4 notes will now be in response to the information provided in the scenario in the Part A set task. The activities in this book can be used in this way. Your notes must also now be in bullet points.**	
	Part A: Reading the brief	p85
	Hints for reading the brief It is stated that you read through the brief and make a list of areas suggested to research. **You will now read through the brief and make notes on the scenario.**	
	Part A: Conducting research	p86
	It is stated that you may conduct research and make notes. **Your notes will now be in response to the information provided in the scenario in Part A.** In the two sample notes extracts on the page, the notes would now need to be formatted **using bullet points**.	

Part B: Small adjustment to example questions on pages 88, 91, 92
Page 88: 2 Provide lifestyle modification techniques (alcohol). **Update: 2 Provide lifestyle modification techniques.**
Page 91: 5 Design key stages of a six-week training programme – week 1. **Update: 5 Design key stages of a six-week training programme.**
Page 92: 6 Provide justification for the training programme that has been produced for the selected individual (week 1). **Update: 6 Provide justification for the training programme that has been produced for the selected individual.**

Answers: update to page 98
Part A: 1 week before assessment task brief (not 2 weeks); 4 A4 sides of **bullet notes in response to the scenario** (not 4 sides of independent research in 8 hours). **Part B:** lasting **2.5 hours** (not 2 hours).

Pearson

REVISE BTEC NATIONAL
Sport

REVISION GUIDE

Series Consultant: Harry Smith

Authors: Sue Hartigan and Kelly Sharp

A note from the publisher

In order to ensure that this resource offers high-quality support for the associated Pearson qualification, it has been through a review process by the awarding body. This process confirms that this resource fully covers the teaching and learning content of the specification or part of a specification at which it is aimed. It also confirms that it demonstrates an appropriate balance between the development of subject skills, knowledge and understanding, in addition to preparation for assessment.

Endorsement does not cover any guidance on assessment activities or processes (e.g. practice questions or advice on how to answer assessment questions), included in the resource nor does it prescribe any particular approach to the teaching or delivery of a related course.

While the publishers have made every attempt to ensure that advice on the qualification and its assessment

is accurate, the official specification and associated assessment guidance materials are the only authoritative source of information and should always be referred to for definitive guidance.

Pearson examiners have not contributed to any sections in this resource relevant to examination papers for which they had prior responsibility.

Examiners will not use endorsed resources as a source of material for any assessment set by Pearson.

Endorsement of a resource does not mean that the resource is required to achieve this Pearson qualification, nor does it mean that it is the only suitable material available to support the qualification, and any resource lists produced by the awarding body shall include this and other appropriate resources.

For the full range of Pearson revision titles across KS2, KS3, GCSE, Functional Skills, AS/A Level and BTEC visit: www.pearsonschools.co.uk/revise

Published by Pearson Education Limited, 80 Strand, London, WC2R 0RL.

www.pearsonschoolsandfecolleges.co.uk

Copies of official specifications for all Edexcel qualifications may be found on the website: www.edexcel.com

Text and illustrations © Pearson Education Limited 2016
Typeset and illustrated by Kamae Design
Produced by Out of House Publishing
Cover illustration by Miriam Sturdee

The rights of Sue Hartigan and Kelly Sharp to be identified as authors of this work have been asserted by them in accordance with the Copyright, Designs and Patents Act 1988.

First published 2016

19 18 17 16
10 9 8 7 6 5 4 3 2

British Library Cataloguing in Publication Data
A catalogue record for this book is available from the British Library

ISBN 978 1 292 15048 2

Printed in the UK by Bell and Bain Ltd, Glasgow

Acknowledgements

We are grateful to the following for permission to reproduce copyright material:

Figures

Figure on page 54 from http://www.bloodpressureuk.org/BloodPressureandyou/Thebasics/Bloodpressurechart, Blood Pressure UK

The author and publisher would like to thank the following individuals and organisations for their kind permission to reproduce their photographs:

(Key: b-bottom; c-centre; l-left; r-right; t-top)

123RF.com: 11b, rido 63, rob3000 23c, zabelin 31c; **Alamy Images:** Colin Edwards 65t, Yon Marsh 17bl; **Corbis**: Ben Blankenburg. 6bl; F**otolia.com**: Galina Barskaya 65, 65b, bergamont 62b, bit24 62t, 62c, Monet 74, whitestorm 61b; **Getty Images**: Paul Bradbury 21t, Echo 10b, Bill Frakes 17br, Fuse 10t, Christopher Futcher 25br, i love images 25bl, Image Source 17bc, Ross Kinnaird 40, Robert Kirk 12bl, Matthew Lewis 27, Jose Luis Pelaez Inc 26t, PhotoAlto / Odilon Dimier 21b, Westend61 25bl (above), 26b; **Image 100**: Corbis / Glow Images 6tr, 8br, 9c, 42; **Pearson Education Ltd**: 15, 22b, 24c, 29t, 30b, 32b, Tudor Photography 6tl, Sozaijiten 6cr (above), 6cr (below), 6br, 39c; **PhotoDisc**: Michael Matisse 5tl, Photolink 9b; **Shutterstock.com**: 29bl, Alila Medical Images 28b, Alila Medical Media 22c, 23b, Alila Medical Media 22c, 23b, Anze Bizjan 19b, Brocreative 12br, Ng Yin Chern 38, CLS Design 15b, Istvan Csak 20, Dionisvera 61t, dotshock 6cl (above), EcoPrint 18b, fotoedu 39t, holbox 12bc, Jiang Dao Hua 3b, ifong 45, ITALO 6cl (below), 77t, Sebastian Kaulitzki 5tr, Lightspring 28t, Maridav 34b, Maxisport 30l, melis 4, Dudarev Mikhail 19t, Christopher Edwin Nuzzaco 34t, Lou Oates 7b, ostill 77b, Edyta Pawlowska 46, Peter Bernik 72, Radu Razvan 39b, Lincoln Rogers 41, ronfromyork 54, Pete Saloutos 36t, Ljupco Smokovski 3tl, 37b, tacar 61c, tankist276 16b, udaix 31b, Valeriy Velikov 66, wavebreakmedia 75, Andrey Yurlov 18c; **Sozaijiten**: 3tr

All other images © Pearson Education

A note from the publisher
In order to ensure that this resource offers high-quality support for the associated Pearson qualification, it has been through a review process by the awarding body. This process confirms that this resource fully covers the teaching and learning content of the specification or part of a specification at which it is aimed. It also confirms that it demonstrates an appropriate balance between the development of subject skills, knowledge and understanding, in addition to preparation for assessment.

Endorsement does not cover any guidance on assessment activities or processes (e.g. practice questions or advice on how to answer assessment questions), included in the resource nor does it prescribe any particular approach to the teaching or delivery of a related course.

While the publishers have made every attempt to ensure that advice on the qualification and its assessment is accurate, the official specification and associated assessment guidance materials are the only authoritative source of information and should always be referred to for definitive guidance.

Pearson examiners have not contributed to any sections in this resource relevant to examination papers for which they have responsibility.

Examiners will not use endorsed resources as a source of material for any assessment set by Pearson.

Endorsement of a resource does not mean that the resource is required to achieve this Pearson qualification, nor does it mean that it is the only suitable material available to support the qualification, and any resource lists produced by the awarding body shall include this and other appropriate resources.

Introduction

Which units should you revise?

This Revision Guide has been designed to support you in preparing for the externally assessed units of your course. Remember that you won't necessarily be studying all the units included here – it will depend on the qualification you are taking.

BTEC National Qualification	Externally assessed units
Certificate	1 Anatomy and Physiology
For both: Extended Certificate Foundation Diploma	1 Anatomy and Physiology 2 Fitness Training and Programming for Health, Sport and Well-being
Diploma	1 Anatomy and Physiology 2 Fitness Training and Programming for Health, Sport and Well-being
For both: Extended Diploma Extended Diploma (HS)	1 Anatomy and Physiology 2 Fitness Training and Programming for Health, Sport and Well-being

Your Revision Guide

Each unit in this Revision Guide contains two types of pages, shown below.

Content pages help you revise the essential content you need to know for each unit.

Skills pages help you prepare for your exam or assessed task. Skills pages have a coloured edge and are shaded in the table of contents.

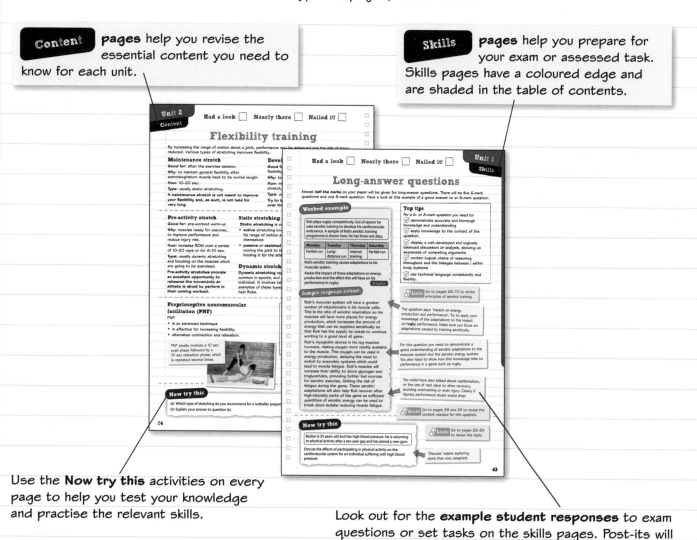

Use the **Now try this** activities on every page to help you test your knowledge and practise the relevant skills.

Look out for the **example student responses** to exam questions or set tasks on the skills pages. Post-its will explain their strengths and weaknesses.

Contents

Workbook also available for externally assessed units ISBN 9781292150475

. . . .

A small bit of small print
Pearson publishes Sample Assessment Material and the Specification on its website. This is the official content and this book should be used in conjunction with it. The questions in *Now try this* have been written to help you test your knowledge and skills. Remember: the real assessment may not look like this.

The skeleton

You need to know the names and locations of the major bones of the axial and appendicular skeleton, and the variations of the curvature of the spine.

Axial skeleton (blue)

The bones of the axial (in blue) and appendicular skeleton (in beige)

Cranium
Cervical vertebrae

Clavicle

Humerus
Rib

Sternum

Scapula
Thoracic vertebrae

Pelvis

Lumbar vertebrae

Radius

Sacrum

Ulna

Carpals
Metacarpals
Phalanges

Femur

Patella

Tibia

Fibula

Tarsals
Metatarsals
Phalanges

Appendicular skeleton (beige)

Neutral spine alignment

Another name for the vertebral column is the spine.

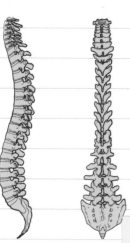

The spine naturally forms an 'S' shape when viewed from the side (in other words there should be three slight curves). When viewed from the back the spine should be straight.

This is neutral spine alignment.

Postural deviations – kyphosis and scoliosis

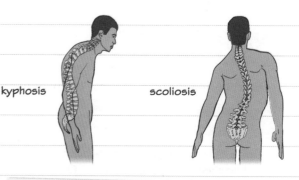

kyphosis   scoliosis

Kyphosis (hunched back) and scoliosis (abnormal sideways curvature of the spine when viewed from the back).

Now try this

(a) Describe the postural deviation kyphosis.

(b) Explain **one** way that the postural deviation kyphosis could impact on performance in sport.

Bone growth

Strong healthy bones are vital for effective sports performance. You will need to know the process of bone growth and the bone cells that enable it to take place.

Process of bone growth

Bone is living tissue. It is formed through a process called **ossification**.

Bone develops in length from infancy to adulthood.

Calcium and phosphate accumulate on the cartilage, trapping it, causing the cells of cartilage to die.

Tiny spaces are left when the cartilage dies. Blood vessels grow in these spaces and transport osteoblasts and nutrients to the developing bone.

The length of your bones can determine your sport. For instance, basketball players are often tall; jockeys, often short.

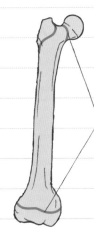

femur

epiphyseal plate (growth plate)

Bone tissue is naturally added at the epiphyseal plate in children and teenagers to increase the length of the bone.

Bone cells

Bone cells comprise:

- **osteoblasts**, which form bone by secreting **collagen**
- **osteoclasts**, which remove bone. Osteoclasts dissolve bone mineral. The degraded bone is then removed.

Growth in diameter of a bone can continue through adulthood.

Bone is continuously being broken down and restructured due to the dynamic relationship between bone cells.

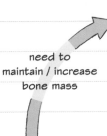

① osteoblasts increase bone matrix

need to maintain / increase bone mass

activity / injury

② micro damage to bone

need for remodelling

③ osteoclasts resorb bone matrix

Sample response extract

Bone mass is maintained through the action of the osteoblasts and osteoclasts. Osteoblasts are responsible for increasing the bone matrix after the osteoclasts have absorbed bone tissue during growth / repair.

Start by identifying the relevant bone cells before describing the role of each.

Now try this

Karl broke his arm playing rugby.

Explain the role of bone cells in Karl's recovery.

Make sure you read each question carefully. Tailor your answer to the question context. The context is a broken arm, so make sure you link your response.

Functions of the skeleton

You need to know the functions of the skeleton and be able to apply your knowledge to a range of different sport and exercise situations.

Supporting framework and movement

The skeleton:

- allows the body to maintain its shape
- allows you to stand erect due to the vertebral column
- provides a framework for muscle attachment
- allows movement due to muscle attachment and the formation of joints between the bones
- allows a vast range of movement from intricate precise movements of the hand to the large range of movement possible at the shoulder.

Leverage

The length of our bones determines our height and the amount of leverage the bones can exert. This will impact on our performance in a range of activities.

It is an advantage for basketball players to be tall.

A tennis player with long arms will be able to exert more force on the ball; improving their service.

Weight bearing

In order to maintain an erect stature, the bones of the pelvis and leg are strong and thick so that they can take the weight of the entire skeleton.

Some other bones are especially designed for strength to allow weight bearing. For instance, the bones at the gymnast's wrists can support her body weight.

Protection

Vital organs are protected from damage due to their position in relation to the bones of the skeleton.

For example:

- the cranium protects the brain
- the vertebrae protect the spinal cord
- the rib cage and sternum protect the lungs and the heart.

Source of blood cell production

The following blood cells develop in the bone marrow:

- red blood cells – important as they carry oxygen to the muscles
- white blood cells – important as they fight infection to keep the performer healthy.

Store of minerals

The bone matrix stores:

- calcium, essential for muscle contraction and bone repair
- phosphorus; too little phosphorus can cause muscle fatigue and joint pain.

The bone marrow stores iron; essential for red blood cell formation.

Now try this

Explain how **two** different bones of the skeleton are used for protection in physical activity.

Give a different sporting example for each bone.

Be clear about how each bone provides protection.

Give examples for **two** different bones in the skeleton, such as the cranium and the ribs.

Bone types

You need to know and understand how each bone type is related to its function and how these functions aid sporting techniques and actions.

Characteristics and examples of bone types

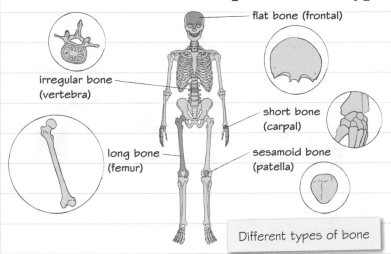

- irregular bone (vertebra)
- flat bone (frontal)
- long bone (femur)
- short bone (carpal)
- sesamoid bone (patella)

Different types of bone

- Long – longer than they are wide, such as the femur, ulna and phalanges
- Short – as short as they are wide, such as the carpals and tarsals
- Flat – broad, flat and normally thin bones, such as the pelvis, sternum and ribs
- Sesamoid – held within tendons, covered in cartilage, such as the patella
- Irregular – irregular shape, such as the vertebrae

Function of long bones

- Source of red blood cells production; essential for oxygen delivery
- Enable large movements, allowing increased speed or range in which an object can be moved
- Act as levers to generate more force on an object

Function of short bones

- Increase stability and reduce unwanted movement
- Are weight bearing; helping the body to remain upright or hold balance
- Absorb shock, such as when running

Function of sesamoid bones

- Ease joint movement, meaning more fluid
- Resist friction so movement is not slowed down

Function of flat bones

- Protect vital organs to reduce injury
- Enable muscle attachment to create movement
- Produce blood cells in adults

Long bone (femur) allows a large movement to increase force as the ball is kicked.

Sesamoid bone (patella) allows ease of movement at the knee.

Flat bone (pelvis) provides large areas for muscle attachment so the hip can be extended to prepare to kick the ball.

Short bones (tarsals) support the body weight so the player remains upright.

Function of the bone types applied to sport.

Now try this

Analyse the role of **one** bone type during a game of badminton.

Think of the roles of the different bone types. For example, a long bone acts a lever – how does this help? What will happen to the speed of the racket? What is the impact of this?

Joint classification

The first thing you need to know is that there are different types of joints in the body.

Types of joints

A joint is formed where two or more bones meet. We classify joints according to the amount of movement they allow.

 Fibrous

These joints are fixed and allow no movement, such as the sacrum and coccyx.

 Cartilaginous

These joints are slightly moveable joints, such as between the lumbar vertebrae.

3 **Synovial**

These are freely moveable joints.

They are important in sport because they provide the greatest range of movement.

The shape of the bones at the joint determines the range of movement. For example, due to the shape of the bones forming the knee, we can only bend and straighten the leg at the knee.

The cranium is also a fibrous joint.

The joints between the cervical and thoracic vertebrae also form cartilaginous joints.

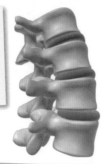

Synovial joints

Synovial joints are divided into six groups based on the amount of movement at each joint.

Condyloid joint

This joint allows movement in two planes.

It allows flexion, extension, adduction, abduction, and circumduction.

Pivot joint

There is a pivot joint at the elbow and between the first and second vertebrae. These joints allow twisting or rotation.

Hinge joint

Examples of these are found at the elbow, knee and ankle.

They allow flexion and extension.

Gliding joint

This joint is formed between the bones of the wrist and foot. The bones glide over each other to allow sliding or twisting movements. For example, the hand action in hockey as you dribble the ball.

Saddle joint

This joint is formed between the carpals and metacarpals at the base of the thumb. The movements are the same as the condyloid joint.

The elbow

Classified as a pivot and hinge joint. This is because there are actually two joints in the area of the elbow. Make sure you know which bones form each joint:

- **pivot** – between the radius and the ulna
- **hinge** – between the radius and the humerus and the ulna and the humerus.

Ball and socket joint

These joints give the greatest range of movement.

Ball and socket joints at the hip and shoulder allow flexion, extension, adduction, abduction and rotation.

Now try this

Go back to page 1 to identify the joints of the upper and lower skeleton.

Analyse how the synovial joints from the upper skeleton allow a player to serve the ball in a game of tennis.

Joints use in sport

You need to understand how the joints of the upper and lower skeleton are used in sporting techniques and actions.

The pivot joint formed between the first and second vertebrae at the neck allows the player to tilt the head back to watch the ball.

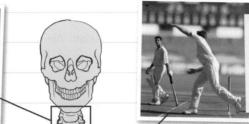

The ball and socket joint formed between the scapula and humerus at the shoulder allows the bowler to bowl the cricket ball.

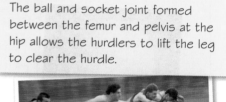

The ball and socket joint formed between the femur and pelvis at the hip allows the hurdlers to lift the leg to clear the hurdle.

The hinge joint formed between the humerus and the radius and ulna at the elbow allows the volleyball player to bend the arm to serve the ball.

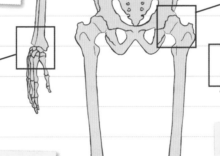

The condyloid joint formed between the radius, ulna and the carpals at the wrist allows the gymnast to put their hand flat on to the bar to maintain their weight.

The saddle joint formed between the carpals and metacarpals at the thumb in the wrist allows the tennis player to grip the racquet and the ball.

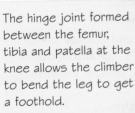

The hinge joint formed between the femur, tibia and patella at the knee allows the climber to bend the leg to get a foothold.

The gliding joint formed between the tarsals and metatarsals of the foot increases the flexibility of the foot, allowing the player to turn the foot to kick the ball.

Now try this

(a) How would the joints between the vertebrae be used in high jump?

(b) The pictures show sporting examples of the use of each type of joint. How else might each of the identified joints be used in sport?

Joint structure

You need to be able to link the function of each component of a synovial joint with its use in sporting techniques and actions.

Components of synovial joints

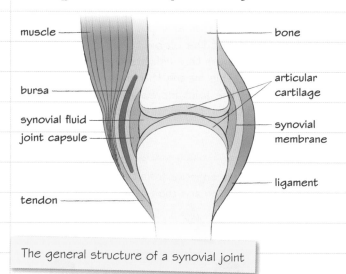

muscle —
bone —
bursa —
synovial fluid —
joint capsule —
articular cartilage —
synovial membrane —
ligament —
tendon —

The general structure of a synovial joint

Function of each component

A joint is formed where two or more **bones** meet. In this example, two bones are meeting to form the synovial joint.

Articular cartilage is a shiny, elastic material, which is designed to reduce friction and absorb shock.

Ligaments connect bone to bone, holding the bones in the correct position. They stabilise the joint.

The **synovial membrane** secretes synovial fluid.

Bursa are found in most major synovial joints. They reduce mechanical friction in the joint. They act as a cushion between bone and another part of the joint, such as tendons or muscles.

Function of each component

The **joint capsule** surrounds the synovial joint. It is attached to the outer layer of the bones forming the joint. It seals the joint and provides stability to the joint.

Synovial fluid:

- lubricates and reduces friction in the joint
- supplies nutrients to the joint
- removes waste products from the joint.

Muscles and tendons

Muscles and tendons are part of the muscular system rather than the skeletal system. They are included on the joint diagram to show they must be present at a joint. Otherwise, there would be no way to move the bones at the joint. The tendon attaches the muscle to the bone and the muscle contracts to bring about movement.

Applied to sporting techniques

The components of the joint aim to keep the joint healthy so that it can continue to function, and you can continue to play sport. The role of the articular cartilage is to protect the bones from wearing out. The bone will be at increased risk of wearing the more you use it. For example, think of the potential wear on the articulating bones at the knee of elite long distance runners who run up to 135 miles in training. Or the importance of the ligaments to maintain the stability of the joint in contact sports such as rugby. The importance of synovial fluid to transport nutrients and lubricate the elbow, (reducing friction at the joint), wrist and shoulder joints of the elite wheelchair athlete who completes 10 miles of road distance training each morning, and sprint training later the same day, is another good example to think about.

An elite wheelchair athlete relies on the components of the elbow joint to maintain its health, so they can continue to put additional stress on it to allow them to train and compete.

Now try this

How would the bursa aid sporting performance in contact activities such as wrestling or judo?

Anatomical position

You need to know about the ranges of movement possible at joints. When describing any movement, it helps to consider the anatomical position. All ranges of movement start, or return, to this position.

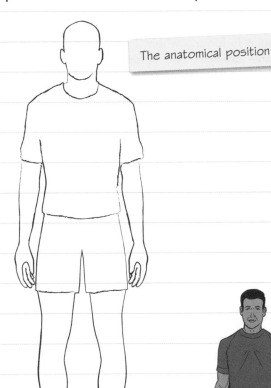

The anatomical position

Flexion, extension

Flexion means reducing the angle of the bones forming the joint (for example, during a bicep curl there is flexion at the elbow to lift or curl the weights). To lower the weights there is extension at the elbow. This means the angle between the bones at the joint increases and the arm is returned to the anatomical position.

Each range of movement has an 'opposite' to allow the limb to move from the anatomical position and then back towards it.

Plantarflexion and dorsiflexion

This range of movement only occurs at the ankle. During dorsiflexion at the ankle the toes are pulled nearer to the lower leg. To move back to the anatomical position, the ankle plantarflexes. The ankle can plantarflex beyond the anatomical position, such as when pointing the toes in a trampolining routine.

The footballer uses dorsiflexion at the ankle to help control the ball, whilst the diver uses plantarflexion to produce a better dive.

Now try this

Name **three** other movements in sport or physical activity that use flexion and extension.

Abduction and adduction

Abduction

Think of a vertical line passing directly through the body from top to bottom. This is known as the midline of the body. A sideways (lateral) movement of the arms at the shoulder, or a sideways movement of the legs at the hip away from the midline is called abduction.

The midline of the anatomical position

The volleyball player is abducting the arm at the shoulder in preparation to serve as he takes the arm sideways away from the body. He is also abducting the leg at the hip as the limb moves away, sideways, from the anatomical position and the midline of the body.

Adduction

Adduction means bringing the bone at the joint closer to the midline of the body, such as returning to a standing position after a martial art kick out to the side of the body, or the recovery phase of the breaststroke leg action.

The gymnast has adducted the legs at the hip to move to a handstand position on the pommel horse.

Horizontal abduction and adduction

Where the word horizontal is added, it simply gives more detail about the movement taking place. Horizontal means from side to side at shoulder height, so **horizontal abduction** means movement away from the midline of the body but horizontally (parallel to the floor) rather than vertically. For instance, when taking a racket back in the preparatory phase of playing a forehand shot in tennis. Horizontal adduction can occur at the hip and the shoulder.

Horizontal adduction occurs at the shoulder as the tennis player moves the arm forward to play the shot. Note how the elbow is facing downwards.

Now try this

(a) What is the difference between adduction and abduction?

(b) Use an example to explain how horizontal abduction differs from abduction.

If someone is abducted they are kidnapped or taken away. Use this meaning of the word to remind you what the range of movement is.

9

Other ranges of movement

These are the remaining ranges of movement you need to know and recognise when used in sporting actions.

Horizontal flexion at the shoulder

This is a very similar movement to horizontal adduction **except** the elbows face out to the sides (forcing the palms to face downwards) as the arms are moved to the midline of the body horizontally. For instance, as a discus thrower brings the arm through to release the discus.

 Links Go to page 9 to revise horizontal abduction and horizontal adduction.

The discus thrower has horizontally extended the arm at the shoulder in preparation to throw the discus. Note the elbow is out to the side.

Horizontal extension at the shoulder

Lateral movement away from the midline of the body horizontally, moving the upper arm away from the chest with elbows at the side. The difference between this movement and horizontal abduction is the position of the upper arm – if the elbow is turned out, it is horizontal extension.

Hyperextension of the spine

Extension of the spine is movement back to the anatomical position. Hyperextension is a continuation of this movement so that the neck moves further away from the chest (cervical vertebrae) or the spine moves away from the pelvis (thoracic and lumbar vertebrae).

Hyperextension of the spine

Lateral flexion of the spine

This is movement away from the midline of the body so the spine moves from side to side. This can occur at the:

- cervical vertebrae, such as moving the neck sideways towards the shoulder as part of a warm-up routine
- thoracic and lumbar vertebrae, such as moving the upper body sideways towards the pelvis when performing a cartwheel.

Circumduction

This is a conical movement. That is, when circumduction occurs at the shoulder the hand will describe a circle, such as the butterfly arm action as the arms leave the water the hands complete a circular action.

Circumduction can occur at the shoulder, wrist, hip and ankle.

Rotation

This is a circular movement that occurs when the bone at the joint turns around an axis. For example, at the elbow and wrist when playing a topspin forehand drive in tennis, or the rotation at the hip during a golf drive.

Now try this

How can you recognise the difference between horizontal flexion and horizontal adduction?

Responses and adaptations

You need to know the short-term responses of the skeletal system to exercise and the resulting long-term adaptions if regular exercise is carried out.

Responses

These are the **immediate, short-term** ways that the skeletal system reacts when you exercise. The reactions are **short lived**. In other words, when you stop exercising the skeletal system has no need to continue to react in this way and therefore stops.

Responses of the skeletal system to exercise

- Stimulates increase of mineral uptake (calcium) within the bones.
- Stimulates production of collagen due to increased stress on bones as a result of exercise.

Responses of the skeletal system to exercise within the joint

Increased range of movement due to:

- reduction in viscosity of the synovial fluid
- increased pliability of the ligaments.

Increased production of synovial fluid to ensure the articular cartilage does not dry out.

Viscosity – how thick liquid is

Adaptations

These are the **long-term** ways that the skeletal system changes due to regular training. These changes are lasting, provided you do not stop **regular** training. In other words, when you stop exercising, the skeletal system does not immediately change back to how it was before the exercise session.

Adaptations of the skeletal system

- Increased bone density and strength due to increased mineral content and bone cell activity make the bones less susceptible to fractures or breaks.
- Increased ligament strength reduce the risk of dislocation at a joint.
- Increased thickness of articular cartilage protects the ends of the bones from wear and tear.

These adaptations reduce the risk of injury making it possible to continue to train or train harder, provided there is adequate rest built in to the programme.

 Links Go to page 2 to revise bone cells and bone growth.

Regular weight-bearing or weight-training exercise makes the areas of the skeleton that are working work harder as they work against gravity, increasing bone strength.

Now try this

Use an example to explain why a warm-up is important to the skeletal system before a hockey match.

When answering a question, make sure you pay attention to the question context and tailor your answer to this, rather than just giving a general response.

Additional factors

You need to understand the potential positive impact of exercise on limiting skeletal disease and the importance to bone growth of waiting until the skeleton has sufficiently matured before taking part in resistance training.

Arthritis

This is a common disease of the skeleton and can affect people of all ages. There are two common types:

- osteoarthritis – mainly develops in those over 40, but can occur at any age
- rheumatoid arthritis – normally develops between the ages of 40–50; women are more susceptible than men to this condition.

However, exercise can delay these conditions by helping the individual maintain a healthy weight and healthy joints.

Types of arthritis

Osteoarthritis causes the articular cartilage to thin, which will cause pain and lack of mobility at the joint. This would make it difficult to continue to exercise.

Rheumatoid arthritis causes inflammation of the joints so they become painful and swollen. The synovial membrane of the joint becomes inflamed, due to a build-up of fluid. Although the inflammation can reduce, the joint capsule has been stretched making the joint less stable. Pain at the joint and, later, the increased risk of deformity at the joint will make activity difficult.

Osteoporosis

This is a reduction in bone density. It can be caused by a lack of calcium, vitamin D and a sedentary lifestyle.

The reduction in bone mass makes the bones more brittle, with increased risk of fracturing a bone from even a minor bump or fall.

Benefits of regular exercise

Higher levels of weight-bearing physical activity can reduce age-related bone loss by putting gentle stress on the bones; not too much that they fracture, but enough so that new bone growth is encouraged.

🔗 Links Go to page 2 to revise bone growth.

Strength training

Whilst strength training can be appropriate for all ages, young children should not engage in weight lifting as it can negatively affect bone growth.

Now try this

(a) Why is arthritis likely to stop you from playing sport?

(b) How can exercise improve bone health?

(c) Why shouldn't young children take part in weight training?

Read every question carefully. Part (c) is about weight training; this is different from strength training.

Muscle types

You need to know the characteristics and functions of the three muscle types and their relevance to sport and physical activity.

Cardiac muscle

Location:
- only found in the walls of the heart.

Function:
- to circulate blood through and out of the heart.

Characteristics:
- unconsciously controlled by the nervous system
- myogenic (has a set rhythm of contraction)
- does not fatigue.

Relevance to sport

The heart keeps the blood circulating, picking up oxygen from the lungs and dropping off waste products. At rest, approximately 5 litres of blood is pumped out of the heart per minute. When we exercise, we have a much greater demand for oxygen and so need to circulate more blood. The cardiac muscle of the heart achieves this by contracting at a quicker rate. Elite endurance athletes can circulate more than 30 litres of blood a minute during exercise. The heart ensures increased oxygen delivery to allow the performer to continue.

2 Skeletal muscle

Location:
- attached to the bones of the skeletal system.

Function:
- movement plus support and posture.

Characteristics:
- consciously controlled
- contract by impulse from brain
- muscle fibres work together in motor units.

Relevance to sport

Without skeletal muscle we would be unable to move our skeleton and therefore unable to participate in sport.

Skeletal muscle is responsible for large body movements such as running, but also precision movements such as a short putt in golf or releasing an arrow in archery.

3 Smooth muscle

Location:
- found in the walls of hollow organs, such as in the digestive and circulatory system.

Function:
- controls body functions, such as movement of food through the body, the passage of urine from the bladder and the movement of blood through the circulatory system.

Characteristics:
- unconsciously controlled by the nervous system.

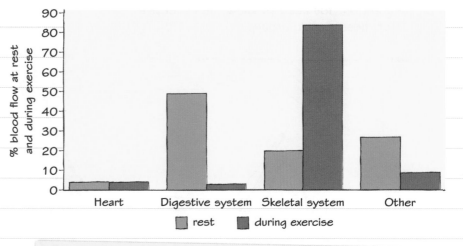

During exercise, the smooth muscle in the blood vessels can restrict or increase blood flow through the blood vessel so that more blood carrying oxygen can go to the skeletal muscle. Therefore performers get the oxygen their muscles need whilst exercising.

Now try this

How does each muscle type aid performance?

 Make sure you know about each muscle type.

The muscular system

You need to know the names and locations of the major skeletal muscles.

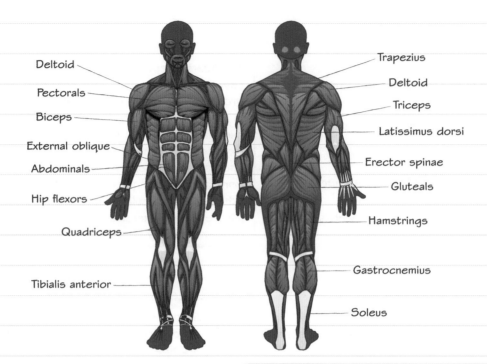

Deltoid
Pectorals
Biceps
External oblique
Abdominals
Hip flexors
Quadriceps
Tibialis anterior

Trapezius
Deltoid
Triceps
Latissimus dorsi
Erector spinae
Gluteals
Hamstrings
Gastrocnemius
Soleus

The names and locations of the major skeletal muscles

Movement of the hand at the wrist

Many different muscles control the movement of the wrist. Some are grouped together based on their action. You need to know the collective names of these muscle groups.

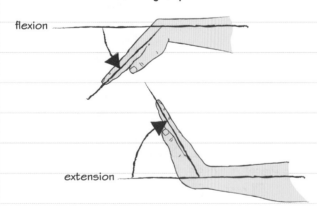

flexion

extension

Wrist flexors and wrist extensors are responsible for flexing and extending the wrist.

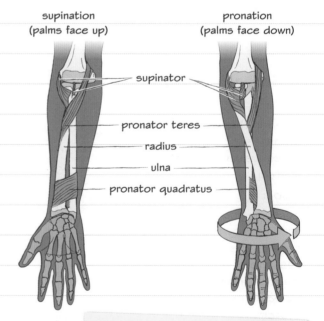

supination
(palms face up)

pronation
(palms face down)

supinator
pronator teres
radius
ulna
pronator quadratus

Supinators turn the palm upwards.
Pronators turn the palm face down.

Now try this

What is the collective name given to the muscles that enable a cricketer to 'cup' their hands (palms up) to catch a ball?

Antagonistic muscle pairs

Muscles work together to bring about movement by taking on different roles, depending on the movement required. You need to know the roles of the muscles and their combined use in a variety of sporting actions.

Muscles work in **antagonistic pairs**. When one muscle in the pair is contracting, the other muscle is relaxing. This is so the full range of movement can be achieved at a joint. The contracting muscle is called the **agonist**, and the relaxing muscle, the **antagonist**. When the movement at the joint needs to be reversed the muscles switch roles, the agonist becomes the antagonist, the antagonist becomes the agonist.

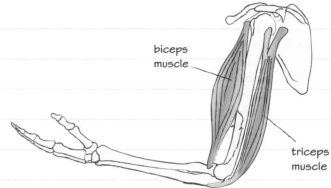

biceps muscle

triceps muscle

The antagonist (triceps) must relax to allow the agonist (biceps) to contract and flex the arm at the elbow. When the arm needs to extend at the elbow, the bicep becomes the antagonist and relaxes, allowing the tricep (now the agonist) to contract.

Synergists

A **synergist** cooperates with the agonist in two ways:

1 Supporting its action by neutralising any undesired action at the joint so that the force generated by the agonist works to bring about the desired action. For example, the latissimus dorsi acts as a synergist for the pectorals when the upper arm is adducted at the shoulder.

2 Assisting the agonist muscle to perform the desired type of movement. For example, the soleus acts as a synergist to the gastrocnemius in dorsiflexion of the ankle.

Fixators

Fixators are muscles that stabilise a joint by eliminating unwanted movement. For example, some of the muscles at the ankle work to stabilise the joint as we stand so that we can balance effectively. During a biceps curl the trapezius will stabilise the movement by preventing the scapula from moving.

The anterior and posterior deltoids work antagonistically to adduct and abduct the arm at the shoulder.

The quadriceps and the hamstrings work antagonistically to allow flexion and extension of the leg at the knee.

The hip flexors and gluteals work antagonistically to allow flexion and extension of the hip.

The tibialis anterior and the gastrocnemius work antagonistically to allow the foot to move from dorsiflexion to plantarflexion.

Now try this

Review the muscles shown on page 14. Identify **five** different antagonistic muscle pairs.

Muscle contraction

You need to know about three different types of muscle contractions. When a muscle contracts, it is working: it is either supporting or moving a load or resistance, or is static under tension.

Concentric contraction

When a muscle contracts and **shortens** it is called a concentric contraction. Concentric contractions are common in power sports or sports where you need explosive force. They cause movement at the joint as the force exerted by the muscle is greater than the resistance. For example, when serving a ball in tennis, the triceps contracts and shortens when you extend the arm to bring the racket through quickly to add pace to the ball.

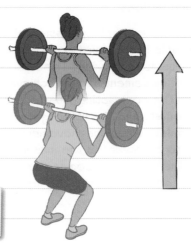

The quadriceps contract concentrically during the **upward** phase of the squat.

Eccentric contraction

When a muscle contracts it can also **lengthen** under a load or tension. This is often when the muscle is working against gravity, trying to control a movement. For example, running down hill or when lowering the body in a press-up the triceps muscle is still working hard to control the rate of descent so that the body doesn't fall to the floor. In this example, the triceps are contracting but lengthening; therefore they are working eccentrically.

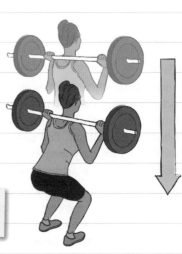

The quadriceps contract eccentrically during the **downward** phase of the squat.

Isometric contraction

When a muscle works isometrically there is little or **no movement** in the muscle or joint. The muscle doesn't shorten or lengthen. For instance, when holding the 'set' position at a sprint start or when weightlifters hold the weights still above their heads for a qualifying lift in the clean and jerk. The muscles are working but there is no movement.

Gymnasts rely on isometric muscle contractions to maintain strength positions on the rings. Their muscles are working but are not shortening or lengthening.

Now try this

Give an example of an exercise activity or technique that would use each type of muscle contraction. Give **one** example for each type of muscle contraction.

Fibre types

You need to know about the different muscle fibre types and their recruitment for a range of exercises and sports.

All or none law

The muscular system works with the nervous system to bring about muscle contraction. Impulses are sent to the muscle via **motor neurones** (nerves). The motor neurone is attached to a number of muscle fibres in the muscle. Together, these are called a **motor unit**. The muscle fibres within a motor unit will be of the same type. When the motor neurone receives the signal to contract, **all** the muscle fibres attached to that neurone will contract (all or none law). The force the muscle produces is altered by adjusting the number of motor units stimulated to contract.

Type I (slow twitch)

Characteristics:

- utilise the aerobic energy system due to dense capillary network and high levels of myoglobin
- contract slowly
- exert the least amount of force of the fibre types
- have the highest resistance to fatigue; allowing the muscles to continue to contract for long periods of time.

Type I fibres are ideal for endurance activities, such as long distance running.

 Links Go to page 35 to revise energy systems.

Type IIa (fast twitch)

Although these are classified as fast twitch fibres, they can develop type I characteristics through endurance training. Therefore, they can utilise either aerobic or anaerobic energy systems depending on the training the performer undertakes. Type IIa fibres have a greater resistance to fatigue than type IIx fibres, but less resistance than type I. They can produce a medium force of contraction. They are ideal for middle distance events.

Type IIx (fast twitch, formerly type IIb)

Characteristics:

- utilise the anaerobic energy system
- produce a strong force of contraction
- consist of larger motor neurones
- the motor units normally have more muscle fibres in them compared to slow twitch motor units
- the muscle fibres tend to be larger and thicker than other fibre types.

These fibre types are ideal for power activities, such as sprinting.

Type I fibres are used in marathon running

Type IIa fibres are used when pace is needed, but over a sustained period of time, such as in squash.

Type IIx fibres are used to generate force to achieve a greater height.

Now try this

How does having a range of muscle fibre types allow 10 000 m runners to perform well in their sport?

Responses

You need to know these five short-term responses of the muscular system to exercise.

Responses

These are the **immediate, short-term** ways that the muscular system reacts when you exercise. The reactions are **short lived**. When you stop exercising, the muscular system has no need to continue to react to exercise, and therefore stops and slowly recovers back to its pre-exercise state.

1 Increased blood supply

During exercise there is an increased need for oxygen to be transported to the working muscles so that energy production is high enough. Oxygen is carried via the red blood cells. The blood supply to the muscles increases by a process called **vascular shunting**. The lumen of the arterioles in the muscles **vasodilates**, to allow an increased passage of blood to the muscles, whilst the arterioles in areas such as the digestive system **vasoconstrict** to reduce blood flow.

 Links Go to page 32 to revise redistribution of blood flow.

Vascular shunting provides the oxygen for exercise.

2 Increased muscle temperature

When we exercise heat is given off as a by-product of energy production. The more intense the level of exercise, the greater the heat produced.

4 Lactate accumulation

Lactate is a by-product of energy production. If enough oxygen is available lactate can be broken down as it is produced. However, as exercise intensity increases lactate builds in the muscles as it is being produced faster than it can be broken down due to insufficient oxygen.

Whatever the sport, exercise will cause temporary changes to the muscular system.

3 Increased muscle pliability

As muscle temperature increases with exercise the muscle becomes more pliable. It has more 'give' so reduces the chance of injury.

5 Microtears

Each muscle is made up of bundles of muscle fibres. Each muscle fibre is made up of bundles of myofibrils. As a result of resistance exercise these myofibrils can sustain microscopic tears, which will need time to repair before exercising the muscle again. These microtears are thought to be the reason for delayed onset of muscle soreness (DOMS).

Now try this

Jermaine is a middle distance runner and Jill is a weightlifter. How would their muscular systems respond to exercise?

Aerobic adaptations

You need to know the **long-term** changes to the muscular system due to regular aerobic training. These changes are lasting, provided you do not stop **regular** aerobic training.

Regular aerobic training includes activities that involve the use of large muscle groups, for example jogging, swimming, cycling, dancing and cross-country skiing.

regular aerobic exercise

→ muscular system adapts due to extra work

body finds it easier to complete exercise

can increase training load as can now work harder for longer

As the muscular system adapts, the aerobic training load can be increased.

Mitochondria

Mitochondria are found in the muscle cells and, with the use of oxygen, generate energy. Regular aerobic training increases the size and number of mitochondria. This means that even more energy can be produced aerobically, allowing the performer to sustain exercise for longer.

Improved use of energy sources

Greater amounts of energy can be released to the muscles for physical work due to increased:

- activity of enzymes that break down our food
- use of glycogen
- use of fat
- stores of glycogen
- stores of triglycerides.

Increased myoglobin content

Myoglobin is similar to haemoglobin, but rather than in the blood it is found in the muscle cells. Its job is to act as an oxygen store in the muscle. With more myoglobin, more oxygen can be transported to the mitochondria, improving aerobic energy production.

Function of adaptations

Most of these adaptations increase the muscles' ability to produce and utilise energy aerobically, in other words, the adaptations allow the performer to work harder, for longer, improving their performance in aerobic, endurance-based activities.

 Links You can revise energy systems on page 35.

Now try this

Becky is often substituted in the final quarter when she plays netball. Explain **one** way aerobic training could reduce the likelihood of Becky being substituted in a netball match.

Anaerobic adaptations

You need to know these five **long-term** changes to the muscular system. These changes are lasting, provided you do not stop **regular** anaerobic training.

Anaerobic training

Adaptations as a result of anaerobic training will target the fast twitch muscle fibres:

- type IIa
- type IIx.

This is because these will be the fibres being used to complete the training. Slow twitch muscle fibres would remain unchanged.

> Muscle hypertrophy of fast twitch fibres can be brought about by resistance training using heavy loads and few repetitions.

 Links You can revise fast twitch fibres on page 17.

① Hypertrophy of fast twitch muscle fibres

As the muscle is stressed during exercise, microtears form in the myofibrils. This stimulates specialised muscle cells called satellite cells to multiply and to fuse with the existing myofibril, helping to repair the damage. As these cells fuse to the existing cells the fibre increases in size rather than generating new fibres. The increased size of the muscle means it becomes stronger and able to apply greater force.

② Increased tendon strength

As the muscles become larger and stronger, the tendons that attach the muscle to the bone also have to adapt so that they can manage the increased force of the contraction of the larger muscle, otherwise the player will become injured. This is achieved by an increase in collagen, adding to the existing collagen fibres that make up the tendon.

③ Increased tolerance to lactate

Lactate threshold is the point at which lactate starts to accumulate in the blood – the moment that the body switches from working aerobically to anaerobically. Therefore, the longer you can remain under this threshold the longer you can use the aerobic energy system. Anaerobic training at about 85 to 90 per cent of maximum heart rate for 30 minutes will improve your body's ability to tolerate lactic acid / lactate (enhancing aerobic performance).

④ Increased energy stores

Increased levels within the muscles of:

- ATP
- PC.

ATP is our way of storing small amounts of energy in the muscle so that it can contract when we need it to. We can break down PC to rebuild ATP once it has been used. By increasing the stores of these, we increase the muscles' ability to work quickly.

⑤ Improved use of energy sources

The muscles get better at breaking down glycogen (even without oxygen) so they can exercise at a high intensity for longer. This is helped by their ability to **buffer** (neutralise) lactic acid more effectively.

> Note the references to energy. The muscular and energy systems work together; the training causes adaptations to both of these systems.

Now try this

Igor uses interval training to improve his time in the 200 metres sprint. Explain **one** way Igor's muscle adaptations to this type of training could help him increase his speed.

Additional factors

You need to understand the additional factors affecting the muscular system and their impact on exercise and performance.

Age

Muscle deteriorates with age. As we get older we lose a percentage of our strength. This varies from person to person, but the average loss of muscle mass is approximately 30 per cent between the age of 50 and 70. The rate of loss increases after this age.

Implications for performance

Loss of muscle is accelerated by a sedentary lifestyle. If we remain active and follow an appropriate strength training programme, the effects of aging can be reduced. Clearly if our performance relies on strength, it will deteriorate due to reduced muscle as we age.

Cramp

Cramp is a sudden, strong contraction of a muscle. It can last for a few seconds or minutes and is very painful. You have no control over the muscle whilst it is experiencing cramp. Because the muscle fibres have contracted and shortened, a hard mass of muscle fibres will form under the skin.

Causes of cramp

Possible causes of cramp include:

☑ overuse of the muscle, such as during extra time in a football match

☑ dehydration, such as a lack of fluid intake during a long run

☑ holding a position for a long time, such as a balance in gymnastics

☑ mineral depletion, such as a lack of calcium in the diet.

It is important, during prolonged activity, to maintain water and mineral balance.

Implications for performance

In order to avoid cramp, performers must make sure they:

- remain hydrated
- maintain an appropriate electrolyte balance.

It is important to maintain the correct level of minerals. Performers need to factor this in to their training and performance, especially if they take part in endurance activities.

It is important to stretch before and after exercise to reduce the risk of cramp. If a performer suffers with cramp during an activity they will need to:

- stop exercising due to the discomfort
- stretch
- massage the affected muscle.

This should relieve the cramp so they are able to start exercising again.

Cramp often occurs in the legs, but can occur in any skeletal muscle.

Now try this

How can you reduce the likelihood of cramp occurring in a long distance race?

The respiratory system

You need to know the names and location of the main components of the respiratory system. These are vital in ensuring we can exercise.

Air is warmed and moistened and dust particles are removed as the air travels through the nasal cavity.

From the trachea the airway splits into a left and right bronchus (bronchi), which further divide into bronchioles.

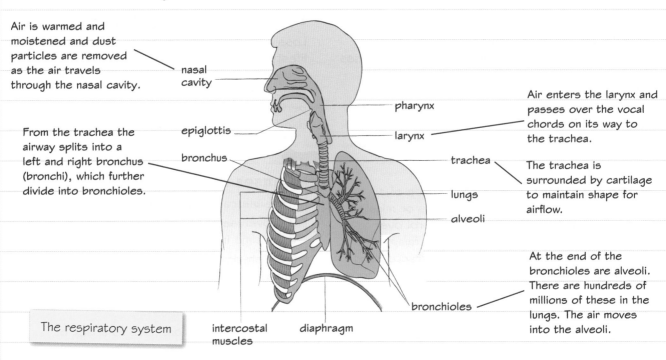

nasal cavity

pharynx

epiglottis

larynx

bronchus

trachea

lungs

alveoli

bronchioles

intercostal muscles

diaphragm

Air enters the larynx and passes over the vocal chords on its way to the trachea.

The trachea is surrounded by cartilage to maintain shape for airflow.

At the end of the bronchioles are alveoli. There are hundreds of millions of these in the lungs. The air moves into the alveoli.

The respiratory system

Bronchiole and alveoli

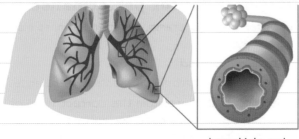

bronchiole and alveolus

Clusters of alveoli are found at the end of each bronchiole.

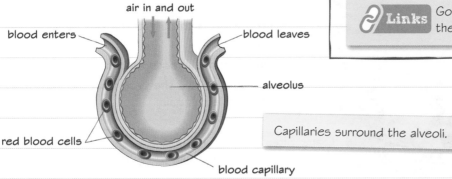

air in and out

blood enters

blood leaves

alveolus

red blood cells

blood capillary

Capillaries surround the alveoli.

The capillaries

The capillaries are part of the cardiovascular system. They work with the alveoli in the respiratory system to make sure that oxygen from the air is transported to the working muscles so that energy can be released for exercise. If there were no way to get air into the body, the cardiovascular system would not have any oxygen to transport and therefore could not release aerobic energy for exercise.

🔗 **Links** Go to pages 28–34 to revise the cardiovascular system.

Now try this

Describe the passage of air through the respiratory system.

Respiratory function

You need to know the function of the respiratory system in supporting exercise and sporting performance.

Thoracic cavity

The thoracic cavity is the area inside the chest from the base of the neck to the diaphragm. It contains the heart and lungs, protected by the ribs and sternum.

The diaphragm and the internal and external intercostal muscles attach to the ribs. Therefore, when these muscles contract they move the rib cage. This means that the volume of the thoracic cavity can be altered.

Inspiration and expiration

During **inspiration**, the thoracic cavity increases in size allowing the lungs to expand and the pressure within them to drop compared to outside. Inspiration causes air to enter the lungs.

During **expiration**, the thoracic cavity decreases in size, reducing the size of the lungs so the pressure increases in the lungs, compared to outside. Expiration causes air to leave the lungs.

Respiration

During inspiration the diaphragm and external intercostal muscles **contract** to increase the area of the thoracic cavity. Note how the diaphragm flattens as it contracts, and how the external intercostal muscles raise the ribs and sternum to allow the lungs to expand.

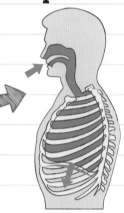

During forced expiration, the diaphragm and external intercostal muscles relax, and the internal intercostal muscles contract. This causes a decrease in the size of the thoracic cavity and lungs.

diaphragm

breathing in:
diaphragm contracts

breathing out:
diaphragm relaxes

Gas exchange

In order to generate energy for sustained activity we need oxygen to get to the muscles. We also need to remove the carbon dioxide that has been produced by the muscles. We need to exchange gases:

- in – oxygen
- out – carbon dioxide.

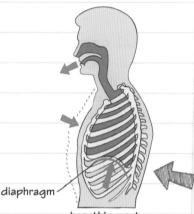

gas exchange

alveolus   tissue cells

O_2 CO_2 O_2 CO_2

Oxygen concentration in the alveolus is high, but it is low in the blood, so the oxygen leaves the area of high concentration for the area of low concentration. Carbon dioxide levels are high in the blood so leave for the alveolus where concentration is lower.

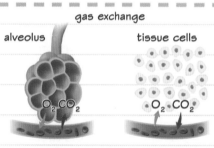

O_2 CO_2 O_2 CO_2

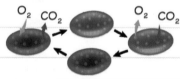

Gases exchange when there is a diffusion gradient; when there is a difference in concentration in one area compared to another. Gas moves from an area of high concentration to low concentration.

Now try this

(a) Why is there a higher concentration of oxygen at the alveolus?

(b) What would you expect to happen to the diffusion gradient during exercise?

Lung volumes

You need to know about the different lung volumes and the changes that occur to some lung volumes in response to exercise and physical activity.

Pulmonary ventilation (VE)

In order to exercise we need oxygen.

↓

We get the oxygen from the air we breathe.

↓

It is the job of the respiratory system to:

↓   ↓

take air into the body   extract some of the oxygen from it.

↓

The process of moving air into and out of the lungs is called pulmonary ventilation.

Lung volumes

You need to be aware of four different lung volumes:

- tidal volume
- vital capacity
- residual volume
- total lung volume.

Each type of lung volume is used to describe the capacity of the lungs at a particular time.

Tidal volume and vital capacity

Tidal volume is the amount of air inspired or expired in a normal breath when the person is at rest. It is the amount of air the person can breathe in or out without forcing their breathing. On average this is 0.5 litres.

Vital capacity is the volume of air that can be inspired or expired per breath, including forced breathing. Vital capacity can be as much as 4.8 litres.

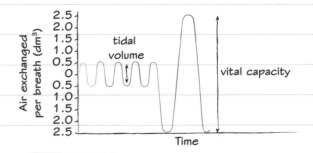

Vital capacity is greater than tidal volume.

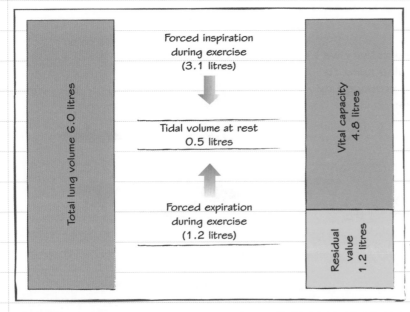

Residual volume and total lung volume

Residual volume is the amount of air left in the lungs even after forced breathing out. This volume of air cannot be breathed out. It prevents the lungs from collapsing. The average residual volume is approximately 1.2 litres.

Total lung volume is vital capacity and residual volume, therefore on average 6.0 litres.

 Lung volumes at rest and during exercise

Now try this

Which lung volumes alter when a performer begins to exercise?

Control of breathing

You need to understand how you control your breathing rate in response to exercise.

Oxygen for energy production

When you exercise you need more oxygen than at rest for increased energy production. Therefore, you need a way to control our breathing rate so that you can:

☑ increase it when you need more oxygen, such as when you exercise

☑ slow it down when there is no longer an increased demand, after you have recovered from exercise.

You control your breathing rate through neural and chemical control.

Links Go to page 23 to revise the role of the diaphragm and intercostal muscles.

The medulla oblongata

- is found in the brain stem, just above the spinal cord
- contains nerve fibres
- is responsible for autonomic nervous activity (i.e. things we do not consciously control such as breathing rate and sneezing)
- is the respiratory centre transferring messages to and from the spinal cord and the brain.

These messages control the action of the diaphragm and intercostal muscles, and therefore the rate of breathing.

The medulla oblongata controls breathing rate based on information from the chemoreceptors.

Medulla oblongata reduces breathing rate.

Rest

Normal breathing rate at rest

Exercise

Chemoreceptors detect drop in CO_2 / increase in pH during recovery.

Chemoreceptors detect increase in CO_2 / drop in pH due to exercise.

Recovery

Medulla oblongata increases breathing rate.

Inspiration and expiration

During inspiration nerve impulses are sent to:

- the external intercostal muscles and
- the diaphragm.

This causes the muscles to contract, increasing the size of the thoracic cavity so that air enters the lungs. During expiration nerve impulses are no longer sent to these muscles, so they stop contracting and relax; decreasing the size of the thoracic cavity.

Adjusting breathing rate

The medulla oblongata knows when to alter breathing rate based on information from the chemoreceptors. Chemoreceptors monitor the chemical content of the blood; in particular, levels of carbon dioxide (CO_2) and the acidity (pH) of the blood.

During exercise, nerve impulses may also be sent to the **internal** intercostal muscles to speed up expiration.

Now try this

Jus and Jo run the 100 metres sprint. After the event their breathing rate is twice as high as it normally is at rest. How was their breathing rate controlled to bring about this increase?

Responses and adaptations

You need to know the short-term responses and long-term adaptations of the respiratory system to exercise.

Impact on sport and exercise performance

The respiratory system responses and adaptations increase oxygen availability and carbon dioxide removal to make participation in physical exercise and sport possible.

Short-term responses

These are the **immediate, short-term** ways that the respiratory system reacts when you exercise. The reactions are **short lived**: when you stop exercising, the respiratory system has no need to continue to react to exercise and therefore stops and slowly recovers back to its pre-exercise state.

1 **Increase in breathing rate**

During normal breathing, whilst at rest, we breathe in and out approximately 12 times per minute, but this can increase to 45 times per minute during intense exercise, or as much as 70 times per minute for an elite athlete.

2 **Increase in tidal volume**

At rest, our tidal volume (air taken in per breath) is approximately 500 ml but this can increase during exercise.

A combination of increased rate of breathing and tidal volume means we can increase the volume of air moving into and out of the lungs from approximately 6 litres per minute at rest to 60 litres per minute whilst performing moderate exercise. This is higher if exercise is more intense.

The increased air means that plenty of oxygen is available for transport to the muscles.

Short-term responses and long-term adaptations provide performers with more oxygen for exercise or a quicker recovery period after exercise.

Long-term adaptations

These are the long-term, sustained changes to the respiratory system resulting from the additional stress placed on the respiratory system due to regular exercise.

1 **Increased strength of the respiratory muscles**

Through increased use, the diaphragm and the external intercostal muscles will become stronger. This means they will be able to contract more forcibly, increasing the size of the thoracic cavity so that a greater volume of air can be taken in to the lungs.

2 **Increased vital capacity**

Due to the increase in size of the thoracic cavity, vital capacity increases.

3 **Increase in oxygen and carbon dioxide diffusion rate**

This is due to an increase in the number of capillaries, as a result of training, allowing more efficient gaseous exchange.

 Links Go to page 24 to revise lung volumes.

Go to page 24 to revise lung volumes.

Now try this

How does the respiratory system respond to a single exercise session?

Unless further detail is given in a question, a 'single exercise session' is a general description of any training session.

Additional factors

You need to understand the additional factors affecting the respiratory system and their impact on exercise and performance.

Asthma

Asthma is a health condition that affects the lungs, in particular, the bronchi. The airways into the lungs are inflamed and easily irritated by a variety of asthma triggers, such as smoke, pollen, dust or stress. When this happens:

- the smooth muscle around the walls of the airways tightens, reducing the size of the airway
- the lining of the airway becomes more inflamed and starts to swell
- phlegm can build up to narrow the airway further.

These reductions in the size of the airway make it difficult to breathe and will lead to wheezing, coughing, tightness in the chest.

Asthma: impact on exercise

✓ Exercise can induce an asthma attack.

✓ There is reduced oxygen delivery to the muscles due to reduction in air getting to the lungs, and a drop in aerobic performance or speed of recovery.

Impact of regular exercise on asthma

The performer would benefit from the training adaptations caused by regular training, in particular:

✓ increased strength of the respiratory muscles

✓ increase in vital capacity

✓ increase in oxygen and carbon dioxide diffusion rate.

All of these would help to reduce the effects of asthma.

Partial pressure

Partial pressure tells us how much of a particular gas is present. Oxygen moves from high pressure (in the alveoli) to low pressure (in the capillaries), until the pressures are equal. Provided the concentration of oxygen is greater in the alveoli than the capillaries, oxygen will leave the lungs for the blood stream. The greater the difference in concentration, the faster the rate of diffusion.

Effects of altitude

At 2400m above sea level we are said to be at high altitude. At high altitude the partial pressure of oxygen is less than at sea level, so, although we will breathe in the same quantity of air, there will be less oxygen available in this air for our bodies to extract and transport to the muscles. As the partial pressure of oxygen drops, the amount of oxygen carried by the haemoglobin in red blood cells also drops.

Altitude: impact on exercise

With less oxygen available, the body cannot work at the same level of intensity, therefore performance levels will drop as athletes will experience muscle fatigue more rapidly.

This is why elite athletes will train at altitude (or mimic training at altitude) before major competitions so that their bodies can adapt, increasing the body's red blood cell count. This allows the athlete to transport more oxygen, off-setting muscle fatigue so they may work harder for longer in aerobic events.

Some elite athletes will train at altitude to improve their ability to work aerobically once back at sea level.

Now try this

Why would sports performers train at altitude before a major competition at altitude?

The cardiovascular system

You need to know the names and location of the main components of the cardiovascular system as these are vital in ensuring we can exercise.

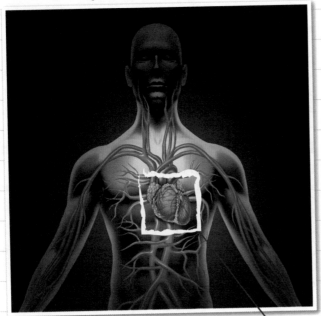

The cardiovascular system

- The cardiovascular system is made up of the heart, blood vessels and the blood.
- Blood is circulated around the body due to the pumping action of the heart.
- The heart is a muscle and therefore requires a blood supply. Blood is transported to the heart muscle via the coronary arteries, which cover the surface of the heart.
- The valves in the heart prevent the backflow of blood within the heart.

Blood flow

Deoxygenated blood passes from the **vena cava** to the **right atrium**. From here it travels through the **tricuspid valve** into the **right ventricle**. Deoxygenated blood leaves the right side of the heart, passing through the **semi-lunar valves** into the **pulmonary artery** to travel to the lungs.

Oxygenated blood from the lungs passes through the **pulmonary vein** to the **left atrium**. From here it travels through the **bicuspid valve** into the **left ventricle**.

Oxygenated blood leaves the left side of the heart, passing through the **semi-lunar valves** into the **aorta** to travel to the body.

The septum divides the heart into left and right sides, keeping the blood in these areas of the heart separated.

Internal anatomy of the heart

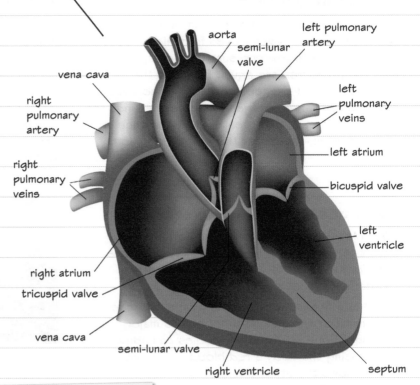

Blood flow is controlled by the pumping of the heart and the use of valves.

Now try this

Describe the passage of blood from the vena cava through the right side of the heart towards the lungs.

Blood and blood vessels

You need to know about the components of blood and the structure and function of the different blood vessels.

Blood

Blood is composed of plasma, red blood cells, white blood cells and platelets. Blood travels around the body through the blood vessels.

Blood vessels

Each type of blood vessel is designed so that it can perform its function effectively. The blood vessel types you need to know are: arteries, arterioles, capillaries, venuoles and veins.

 Arteries:

- always carry blood **away** from the heart
- always carry oxygenated blood, with the **exception** of the pulmonary artery, which takes deoxygenated blood away from the heart to the lungs
- are elastic, so they can accommodate changing volumes of blood passing through them
- have muscular walls that can contract to maintain blood pressure when there is a reduction in blood flow.

 Arterioles

Arterioles link arteries with capillaries. They have similar properties and functions to arteries. However, they have thinner muscular walls as blood is not at such a high pressure as they are further from the force of contraction of the heart. Their muscular walls allow the arteriole to control blood flow into the capillary, vasodilating to increase blood flow during exercise and vasoconstricting to reduce blood flow when resting.

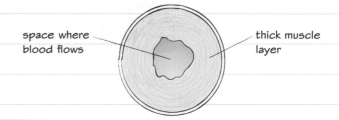

space where blood flows   thick muscle layer

Arteries have thick muscular walls as the blood they carry is at high pressure. The pressure of the blood is high as it has just been expelled from the heart.

 Links Go to page 30 to revise vasoconstriction and vasodilation.

 Capillaries

Capillaries are one cell thick, allowing exchange of gases, nutrients and waste products between the blood in the capillary and the surrounding tissue. Blood pressure in the capillary is lower than in arterioles, but higher than venuoles.

Capillaries link the arterioles and venuoles.

 Venuoles

Although small, these are larger than capillaries. They carry deoxygenated blood and take the carbon dioxide from the capillary and transport it to the veins.

 Veins

Return deoxygenated blood to the heart (with the exception of the pulmonary vein, which carries oxygenated blood). Blood flows slowly through veins. Blood is moved along the vein via the skeletal-muscle pump.

outer layer   valve

Blood in veins is under low pressure so they need valves to stop the back flow of blood.

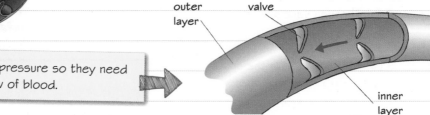

inner layer

 **Now try this**

Which type of blood vessel controls blood flow to the capillaries?

Functions of the cardiovascular system

Many of the functions of the cardiovascular system are carried out by the components of the blood. You need to know the function of plasma, red blood cells, white blood cells and platelets, and how they support sport and exercise performance.

The functions of the cardiovascular system are:

- the delivery and removal of nutrients and waste
- thermoregulation
- vasodilation and vasoconstriction
- to clot blood
- to fight infection.

Plasma is needed to transport essential nutrients to the muscles so there is energy for exercise.

Functions of the blood

Plasma is the liquid part of blood. It is 90 per cent water. Plasma makes it possible to carry the blood cells, nutrients, gases and waste products around the body. Without plasma, these rugby players would not be able to:

- circulate the required oxygen, carried by the red blood cells, that is vital in energy production for exercise
- transport carbon dioxide and lactate, produced during exercise. Carbon dioxide is transported to the lungs to be breathed out of the body. Lactate is transported to the liver.

White blood cells

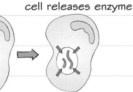

membrane folds around the bacteria

cell releases enzyme

white blood cells can change their shape and wrap around bacteria

once inside the white blood cell, enzymes are released to digest the bacteria

White blood cells keep the performer healthy by fighting infection so they do not need a break from training.

Platelets

Platelets prevent blood loss. During contact sports such as rugby and boxing, players may receive a cut. Blood will flow from a cut until the site is blocked. Platelets will gather, sticking to each other to form a plug at the site of the injury. The platelets also stimulate fibrin (a blood protein) to form a sticky net trapping red and white blood cells, so a clot is formed and the skin is resealed, stopping blood loss. As soon as blood loss is stopped, the player is allowed to re-join the game.

Thermoregulation

It is important that we keep our body temperature at, or close to, 37°C. This is so the reactions in our body, for example those required for energy production, can work at an optimum level. During exercise, when we need efficient energy production, we generate heat. The cardiovascular system helps us lose this excess heat through vasodilation.

The vessels do not move or increase in size; it is the space within the vessel that alters.

Vasoconstriction and vasodilation

Smooth muscle in the walls of the arterioles near to the surface of the skin relax, causing the arteriole to vasodilate. This increases blood flow through these vessels so that a greater amount of blood can pass near the skin and lose heat.

If we need to maintain heat, for example, if exercising in a cold environment, the blood vessels near the surface of the skin will vasoconstrict, reducing blood flow and heat loss.

Now try this

State **four** functions of the cardiovascular system.

Cardiac cycle

You need to know about the cardiac cycle and its control to allow changes in heart rate during sport and exercise.

Blood movement through the heart

Blood movement through the heart is controlled by muscular contraction of the walls of the chambers of the heart and one-way valves.

The atria contract, forcing blood through the bicuspid and tricuspid valves, into the ventricles, which are relaxing so they can fill with blood. This is diastole.

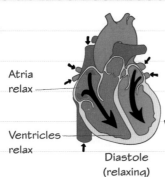

Atria relax

Ventricles relax

Diastole (relaxing)

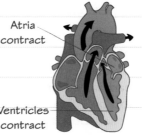

Atria contract

Ventricles contract

Systole (contracting)

The atria relax, the bicuspid and tricuspid valves close, the ventricles contract, forcing blood through the semi-lunar valves, out of the heart into the main arteries (the pulmonary artery or aorta). This is systole. During this time the atria are refilling with blood for the next cardiac cycle.

Cardiac cycle is the term given to the events that take place in the heart each time the heart beats. It includes diastole and systole.

Varying the cardiac cycle

Each heartbeat contains a cardiac cycle. The rate the heart beats is controlled by the nervous system. We need to regulate our heartbeat so our cardiovascular system can carry out its functions. The sympathetic nervous system causes the heart to increase during exercise, after exercise the heart rate slows down due to the parasympathetic nervous system.

We need to be able to vary heart rate depending on the intensity of exercise.

Control of the cardiac cycle

The sinoatrial node acts as a pacemaker; it initiates the heartbeat. It transmits electrical impulses causing the atria to contract. Each electrical impulse is detected by the atrioventricular node and passed to specialised cardiac muscle fibres called the bundle of His. These muscle fibres conduct the impulse throughout the muscular walls of the ventricles. The Purkinje fibres receive these electrical impulses and signal both ventricles to contract.

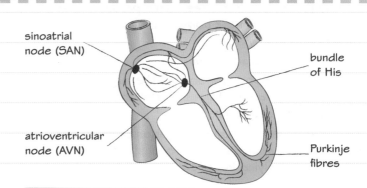

sinoatrial node (SAN)

bundle of His

atrioventricular node (AVN)

Purkinje fibres

The sympathetic nervous system sends messages to the SAN to increase heart rate, for example during exercise.

Now try this

What effects do the sympathetic and parasympathetic nervous systems have on heart rate?

Responses

You need to know these five short-term responses of the cardiovascular system to exercise.

Changes in heart rate when exercising

- **Anticipatory rise** – an increase in heart rate just before the start of physical activity. It is caused by the release of adrenalin into the blood.
- **Increased heart rate** – to speed up oxygen delivery and carbon dioxide removal during exercise.

Increased blood pressure

Blood will be flowing at a faster rate due to the increase in heart rate. Also, the heart will contract more forcibly to squeeze more blood out. This will cause a temporary increase in systolic blood pressure.

🔗 **Links** Go to page 34 to revise blood pressure.

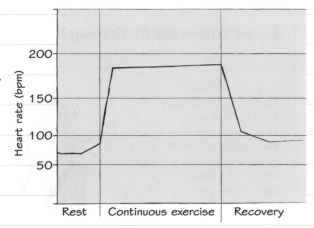

Resting, working and recovery heart rates, before, during and after exercise.

Increased cardiac output

Cardiac output is the amount of blood leaving the heart per minute. It is calculated by multiplying heart rate by stroke volume.

Stroke volume is the amount of blood leaving the heart per beat. If either heart rate or stroke volume increase, cardiac output will increase.

Redirection of blood flow

When we exercise we need more oxygen for greater energy production. This increase in energy production increases waste products that need removing from the body. The body satisfies these demands by:

- increasing cardiac output
- redirecting blood flow so that the majority of the circulating blood goes to the areas of the body that need it most.

This is achieved through vasodilation of arterioles supplying active areas and vasoconstriction of arterioles supplying inactive areas.

🔗 **Links** Go to page 30 to revise vasoconstriction and vasodilation.

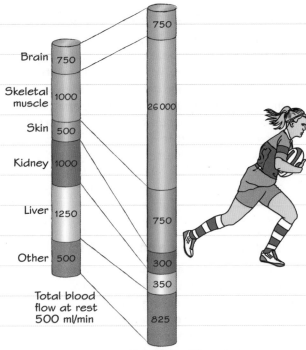

	Total blood flow at rest 500 ml/min	Total blood flow during strenuous exercise 29 975 ml/min
Brain	750	750
Skeletal muscle	1000	26 000
Skin	500	750
Kidney	1000	300
Liver	1250	350
Other	500	825

Increased cardiac output and redirection of blood flow allows a much greater flow of blood to the working muscles during exercise.

Now try this

Why does the body redirect blood flow during exercise?

Adaptations

You need to know the long-term adaptations of the cardiovascular system to regular exercise and the impact of these adaptations on subsequent performance.

1 Cardiac hypertrophy

Hypertrophy means muscle cell enlargement, i.e. an increase in the size of a muscle. Cardiac hypertrophy means this increase is taking place in heart muscle.

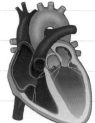 

Untrained heart   Cardiac hypertrophy

Cardiac hypertrophy will increase the thickness of the left ventricle wall, allowing the heart to contract with greater force.

2 Stroke volume increases

Stroke volume increases as the muscular walls of the heart undergo cardiac hypertrophy. Therefore, more blood can be ejected from the heart per beat. This is true at rest and during exercise.

3 Resting heart decreases

If we increase our resting stroke volume, we do not need the heart to beat as often to achieve the required cardiac output at rest.

4 Decreased heart rate recovery time

Heart rate remains elevated after exercise to aid recovery. However, due to an increased stroke volume, a high level of blood can still be circulated without the need for a very high heart rate. Therefore, heart rate will return to resting levels sooner.

5 Capillarisation

This is the development of the capillary network in the body. Capillary density is increased in skeletal muscle and around the alveoli in the lungs. The increase in capillary density means that a greater volume of blood can flow through the body, ensuring a good supply of oxygen and nutrients to the tissues, and removal of carbon dioxide.

7 Reduction in resting blood pressure

This is one of the reasons why exercise is said to be good for us. By dropping resting blood pressure, we reduce the risk of heart-related ill health. Several factors contribute to a drop in resting blood pressure:

- cardiac hypertrophy
- increased nitric oxide release, which vasodilates the blood vessels
- increased plasma volume.

6 Increase in blood volume

Blood volume is a measure of the amount of plasma and red blood cells circulating around the body. Initial increases in blood volume are due to an increase in plasma, although maintenance of training can also result in an increase in red blood cells. The increase in blood volume improves oxygen delivery and temperature regulation.

As the volume of blood plasma increases to a greater extent than the number of red blood cells within it, the viscosity of the blood will not increase; it may even reduce. If blood viscosity does reduce it will decrease its resistance to blood flow, therefore contributing to a reduction in resting blood pressure.

Viscosity – how thick a liquid is.

Now try this

Why does resting heart rate decrease if resting stroke volume increases?

Additional factors

You need to understand the additional factors affecting the cardiovascular system and their impact on exercise and performance.

Sudden arrhythmic death syndrome (SADS)

SADS, results in sudden death, normally in people under the age of 35. It is caused by cardiac arrhythmia. Cardiac arrhythmia is a condition caused by an irregular heartbeat, it means that the normal rhythm of the heart is altered causing cardiac arrest.

Most cases of cardiac arrhythmia do not result in sudden death. However, as there are often no clear symptoms of SADS people are likely to have the condition, and not know. When these people participate in strenuous exercise, even though they appear fit and healthy, they can die due to SADS.

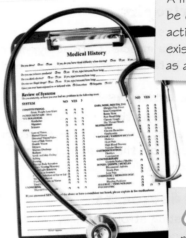

A medical history form should be completed before increasing activity level. This checks for existing health conditions such as a family history of SADS.

Links Go to page 31 to revise nervous control of the heart.

Blood pressure

As blood passes through the blood vessels it exerts a pressure against the walls of the blood vessel.

The amount of pressure exerted will vary depending on:

☑ the rate of blood flow

☑ the size of the internal diameter of the blood vessel.

The faster the blood flows, and the less space available to flow in, the greater the blood pressure.

Blood pressure readings

Blood pressure is expressed as two figures. **Systolic**, when the heart contracts and **diastolic**, when the heart is relaxing.

- normal blood pressure – 120/80 mmHg
- high blood pressure (hypertension) – 140/90 mmHg
- low blood pressure (hypotension) – 90/60 mmHg.

High blood pressure increases the risk of heart attack or stroke. Exercise increases blood pressure during the activity.

Hyperthermia

Hyperthermia is an increase in core body temperature. It can lead to heat cramps, heat exhaustion or heat stroke. When we exercise, we generate heat, which we can normally lose through thermoregulation. However, if we are in a hot environment this becomes more difficult, although appropriate clothing can help.

Links Go to page 30 to revise thermoregulation.

Hypothermia

Hypothermia is a drop in core body temperature below 35°C. It can occur when exposed to cold, or cold and wet conditions for long periods of time without adequate clothing. In these conditions performers will lose their ability to make decisions or move quickly.

Now try this

Why is it important to complete a medical history questionnaire when joining a new sports or fitness club?

The role of ATP

You need to understand the role of ATP for muscle contraction for exercise and sports performance.

Energy

Energy cannot be created or destroyed, but we can change its form. The fats and carbohydrates we eat contain energy. They are our food fuel sources. Once eaten, our body begins to digest these foods, breaking them down into useable forms of energy.

Energy systems

There are three energy systems: ATP-PC, lactic acid system and aerobic system.

Each works in a slightly different way to produce energy from our food fuel sources. All three systems resynthesise (rebuild) ATP.

ATP

ATP is the accepted abbreviation for adenosine tri-phosphate. It is the chemical form of energy that our body uses for all muscle contractions. Without ATP we would have no energy for movement. A small store of ATP is found in muscle cells so that it is available instantly. It is an immediately accessible form of energy for exercise. ATP stores in the muscle last for approximately two to three seconds so the body needs to find a way to resynthesise ATP so we can work for longer. It does this by using one of the three energy systems.

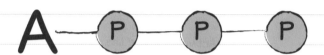

ATP is made up of one molecule of adenosine and three molecules of phosphate. A for adenosine, T for tri (meaning three), and P for phosphate. Each molecule is bound to another as shown by the blue line.

ADP means adenosine di-phosphate. Di means two.

Breakdown of ATP for muscle contraction

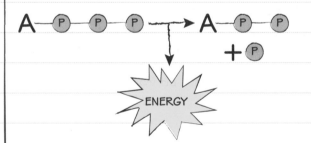

The bond joining the final phosphate in the ATP chain breaks, releasing energy, ADP and a single phosphate.

Resynthesis of ATP for future muscle contraction

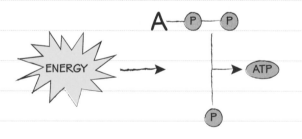

Energy is provided by one of the three energy systems to rebuild the bond between ADP and a single phosphate to resynthesise ATP.

Now try this

(a) What is ADP?

(b) How long does ATP last in the muscle?

(c) What are the three energy systems used to resynthesise ATP?

The ATP-PC system

You need to understand the role of the ATP-PC system in energy production for exercise and sports performance.

Aerobic and anaerobic activity

Sport and exercise activities are often described as aerobic, anaerobic or a mixture of both. This relates to how much the sport or exercise activity relies on the presence of oxygen for energy production. Those activities requiring oxygen are said to be aerobic, those that depend on energy production without the presence of oxygen are said to be anaerobic.

Activities where the performer needs to jump or sprint are anaerobic activities.

Anaerobic activities

These types of activities:

- ✓ are short in duration
- ✓ require the use of fast twitch muscle fibres
- ✓ rely on strength, speed or power.

ATP-PC

ATP is the chemical form of energy that our body uses for all muscle contractions. There is sufficient ATP in the muscles for approximately 2–3 seconds of work; after this more ATP needs resynthesising (rebuilding). In the ATP-PC system the energy required to resynthesise ATP is provided by phosphocreatine (PC).

PC is made up of a molecule of phosphate and a molecule of creatine. There is enough PC in the muscle cell to continue to resynthesise ATP for approximately 8–10 seconds of physical work.

Advantages / disadvantages

The advantages of this system are that energy is released quickly and no waste products are formed. The disadvantages are the limited stores of PC and the 2–3 minutes required to fully recover these stores. This means there is insufficient recovery time during play in many sporting situations to recover the PC stores once they have been used.

Recovery time

Once the supply of PC has been broken down to resynthesise ATP, energy is needed from another energy system to resynthesise the PC stores. This energy is provided from the aerobic system.

The chemical bond between the phosphate and creatine molecule breaks, releasing energy that is then used to resynthesise ATP.

Now try this

What type of activity would allow performers a 2–3 minute rest so they could use the PC system again during their competition?

The lactate system

You need to understand the role of the lactate system in energy production for exercise and sports performance.

The lactate system

The lactate system of energy production is anaerobic. This means that oxygen is **not** used in the process. This system produces energy relatively quickly, so it is good for short-duration, high-intensity activities.

The food fuel source carbohydrate is broken down by the body to form glucose. Some of this glucose goes into the blood stream, some is converted to glycogen and stored in the muscle cells and liver.

Anaerobic glycolysis

Glucose and glycogen are partially broken down by the lactate system to produce ATP.

ATP is used in this breakdown, but more ATP is produced than used, each molecule of glucose produces two net (additional) molecules of ATP.

Energy can be supplied by the lactate system for approximately 1–2 minutes of intense activity.

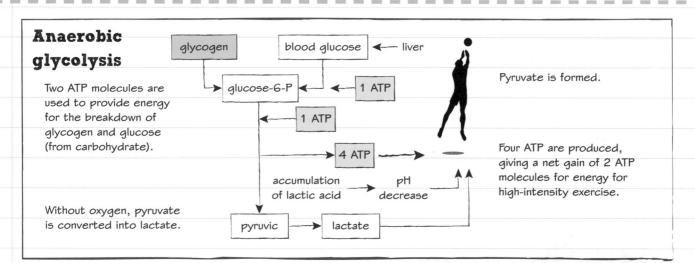

Anaerobic glycolysis

Two ATP molecules are used to provide energy for the breakdown of glycogen and glucose (from carbohydrate).

Without oxygen, pyruvate is converted into lactate.

glycogen → blood glucose ← liver

glucose-6-P ← 1 ATP

1 ATP

4 ATP

accumulation of lactic acid → pH decrease

pyruvic → lactate

Pyruvate is formed.

Four ATP are produced, giving a net gain of 2 ATP molecules for energy for high-intensity exercise.

Recovery

The lactate produced through this system will accumulate unless there is oxygen available to break it down. As the lactate accumulates it changes the acidity of the blood, reducing the efficiency of muscle contraction, causing muscle fatigue. Therefore, this system can only be used maximally for 1–2 minutes before requiring recovery. A recovery time of approximately 8 minutes will aid the removal of lactate from the muscles and also give time to replace the glycogen stores in the muscles.

 Links Go to page 18 to revise lactate accumulation.

The lactate system is used in anaerobic activities that last under 3 minutes but are performed at high intensity, for example a 400 m run or an uphill climb in a cycling race.

Now try this

(a) What is the name of the by-product of anaerobic glycolysis that can lead to muscle fatigue?

(b) Why does this by-product cause muscle fatigue?

The aerobic system

You need to understand the role of the aerobic energy system in energy production for exercise and sports performance.

Aerobic energy production

The aerobic system uses oxygen in energy production. The advantage of this is that it yields large numbers of ATP molecules compared to either of the anaerobic energy systems. This makes it ideal to provide energy for endurance activities. The disadvantage of this system is that releasing the larger quantities of energy involves more chemical reactions. This makes the system slower, and unsuitable for anaerobic activity as it cannot produce the required amount of energy quickly enough for intense activity.

Endurance activities such as long distance cycling, running or swimming rely on the aerobic system for energy production.

 Links Go to pages 36 and 37 to revise anaerobic energy production.

The aerobic system

Stored fats and carbohydrates are used as the fuel source for this energy system. They are broken down into glycogen, glucose and fatty acids. There are three main processes within this system.

1 Glycolysis: this is identical to anaerobic glycolysis (see page 37). However, due to the presence of oxygen, pyruvate is broken down later in the process rather than forming lactate. Two net ATP molecules are produced.

2 Krebs cycle (or citric acid cycle) takes place in the mitochondria (see page 19). The pyruvate from anaerobic glycolysis forms Acetyl-CoA, which is broken down, using oxygen to form carbon dioxide and hydrogen. Two ATP molecules are released.

3 Electron transport chain, which is the final part of the process. Hydrogen from Krebs cycle combines with oxygen to form H_2O as a waste product, and 34 molecules of ATP are produced.

Recovery time

The time required for recovery of this system can be a few hours or as long as 2–3 days, depending on the intensity and duration of the exercise and your level of fitness. For example, after a marathon, it may take 2–3 days before your body is ready to run this type of event again.

Energy for exercise

Each energy system is used to generate energy for physical activity. The amount used will depend on the intensity and duration of the activity. For example, in a game of football, the aerobic system provides energy for the majority of the match. However, when a short sprint, a powerful kick or explosive jump is required, one of the anaerobic systems will be used. During a quiet spell in the game where intensity is low the anaerobic systems can be partially recovered from the aerobic system.

Now try this

Why is the aerobic system suited to low-intensity, long-duration activities?

Make sure you consider both parts of the question, low-intensity and long-duration.

Adaptations

Regular training will cause adaptations to the energy systems involved in that training. You need to know what the energy system adaptations are and the impact these have on exercise and sports performance.

ATP-PC system adaptations

The ATP-PC system resynthesises ATP through the breakdown of phosphocreatine (PC). Although a very fast energy production system, it is limited by the stores of PC. If the body is able to store more creatine this will allow the ATP-PC system to be used for longer.

A sprinter will be able to delay deceleration in a race, improving their sprint time. →

Lactate system adaptations

The lactate system is anaerobic, so produces lactate as a by-product of energy production. Lactate, if left to accumulate, can cause muscle fatigue. This system adapts by building up a tolerance to lactic acid, therefore the muscles do not become fatigued as quickly, extending the length of time this energy system can be used for before needing recovery.

A 400 m runner is able to continue to work at high intensity for longer due to an increased tolerance to lactate. Therefore, they can run faster and for longer, improving their race time.

Aerobic system adaptations

There are three main adaptations:

1 increased ability to use fats as a food fuel source

2 increased storage of glycogen

3 increased number of mitochondria.

Each of these adaptations increases our potential for aerobic energy production. With more fuel available and more sites to break down this fuel aerobically, energy production will be more efficient. This will allow performers to maintain a high level of performance for longer before fatiguing, or a quicker recovery between performances.

Adaptations to the aerobic system allows performers to participate in extreme endurance events, such as the Tour de France where cyclists race approximately 2200 miles in three weeks.

Now try this

(a) How does the aerobic system adapt as a result of long-term training?

(b) Why is this an advantage to the performer?

Additional factors

You need to understand the additional factors affecting the energy systems and their impact on exercise and performance.

Diabetes

Diabetes is a common health condition. It is caused by the body's inability to regulate the amount of glucose in the blood.

There is a lack of insulin, or insulin function, so glucose remains in the blood rather than travelling into the cells.

This means blood glucose is too high, and there is insufficient glucose in the cells.

Therefore, diabetes impacts on the amount of energy we can use from the food fuel carbohydrate.

Types of diabetes

 Type 1 diabetes

This occurs when the body is not able to produce insulin. As the body cannot get energy from glucose it looks elsewhere, breaking down fat and protein. Although those with diabetes are encouraged to exercise, energy production would be limited to the ATP-PC system and the aerobic system unless insulin is injected into the body, or an insulin pump is used.

 Type 2 diabetes

This is the more common form of diabetes. It develops when not enough insulin is produced by the body, or when insulin is present but is not carrying out its function.

Hypoglycaemic attack

This is when blood sugar falls too low. Although encouraged, participation in sport can increase the risk of having an attack. This is why people with diabetes must monitor glucose levels before and after activity. Those on insulin may need to eat carbohydrates before exercise, during or after to help balance their blood glucose.

Diabetes need not impact on sport performance. For example, Sir Steve Redgrave was managing type 2 diabetes when he won his fifth Olympic Gold medal for rowing.

Implications for performance

Different sports will have different effects on blood sugar levels. For example, aerobic activity can lower blood glucose, but anaerobic activities can increase it. Having too high or too low blood glucose will negatively affect energy levels and therefore performance.

The lactate system in children

This energy system is still developing during childhood, and is not fully developed until around 20 years. This is due to:

- lack of muscle mass
- lower glycogen stores
- fewer essential enzymes required for energy production.

Implications for performance

- Children would not gain much from training anaerobically as their lactate system would not be able to adapt to the training.
- Children are better suited to aerobic exercise as their bodies can adapt and make improvements.

Now try this

Why is it important if you have diabetes to monitor your blood glucose levels before and after activity?

About your Unit 1 assessment

You will have 1 hour 30 minutes to complete the Unit 1 exam paper. You need to answer **every question**.

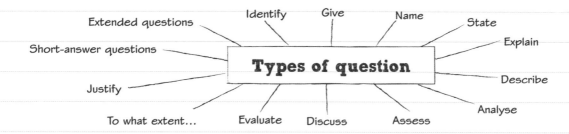

Extended questions

Short-answer questions

Justify

To what extent...

Identify   Give   Name   State

Explain

Types of question

Describe

Analyse

Evaluate   Discuss   Assess

Number of marks

The paper is worth 90 marks in total. The marks are shown in brackets. Marks will range from 1 mark to 8 marks. The number of marks indicate the amount of time you should spend on each question.

1 mark = 1 minute

The amount of writing space available will give you an idea of how much detail is needed in each of your answers.

Remember to take a **black** ballpoint into your assessment. It's a good idea to have a spare pen as well.

Worked example

Nasreen is training for a marathon.

Explain one adaptation to Nasreen's aerobic energy system that could improve her marathon running performance. **3 marks**

This question is worth 3 marks. You should aim to spend no more than 3 minutes answering this question.

Sample response extract

Nasreen will have an increased ability to use fats as an energy source. This will be important to her as she will need to keep running for several hours to complete the race. Without sufficient energy she will have to reduce her pace, possibly stopping altogether. With access to additional fats she will be able to run further for longer, improving her time.

This is an **'explain'** question. You need to show that you understand the topic and give reasons to support your opinion or argument. Make sure you give enough detail to justify your answer.

 Links Go to pages 38 and 39 to revise the content covered in this question.

Now try this

Describe how ATP can be used in energy production for physical activity.

This question asks for a description. You do not need to supply a reason in your answer, just give an account of the stages that occur.

Links Go to page 35 to revise this topic.

Command words

Most of the questions on your exam will be short-answer questions, requiring a limited number of statements or sentences. Most short-answer questions will be between 1 to 4 marks. A variety of command words will be used in these questions.

Give, name, state, identify, describe

These types of questions are asking for knowledge about a body system, for example, its structure or function, or your ability to apply your knowledge.

> As the command word is 'state', you do not need to give an explanation, just the name of the muscle responsible for the action.

Worked example

Marvin used free weights to bicep curl as part of his strength training programme.

State the name of the muscle contracting continually during the biceps curl. `1 mark`

Sample response extract

The biceps.

Analyse, assess

These command words are often more demanding, requiring you to look at something in detail, such as the impact of a type of training on a body system, or an analysis of movement.

> As the command word is 'analyse' you must make sure you use the photo, breaking down the movement, identifying how the antagonistic pair work together to allow the diver to achieve the required shape.

> This question could easily be extended to six marks by asking about more antagonistic muscle pairs or joint actions.

Worked example

Analyse how the antagonistic muscle pair at the hip allow the diver to achieve the position shown. `3 marks`

Sample response extract

The muscle pair operating at the hip are the hip flexors and the gluteals. To achieve this shape, the hip flexors are the agonists, contracting to cause flexion at the hip, but this is only possible if the gluteals relax, taking on the role of the antagonistic muscle.

Evaluate, to what extent

These command words require a judgement based on your knowledge or the information presented in the question and a conclusion. They are used in long-answer questions.

Graphs and data

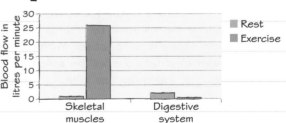

Now try this

Using the graph, explain the changes in blood flow to the muscles and digestive system during physical activity.

> Use the information in the graph to help you. Clearly there is an increase in blood flow to the skeletal muscles. Why do we need this increased blood flow during exercise?

Long-answer questions

Almost **half the marks** on your paper will be given for long-answer questions. There will be five 6-mark questions and one 8-mark question. Have a look at this example of a good answer to an 8-mark question.

Worked example

Rob plays rugby competitively. Out of season he uses aerobic training to develop his cardiovascular endurance. A sample of Rob's aerobic training programme is shown here. He has three rest days.

Monday	Tuesday	Thursday	Saturday
Fartlek run	Long-distance run	Interval training	Fartlek run

Rob's aerobic training causes adaptations to his muscular system.

Assess the impact of these adaptations on energy production and the effect this will have on his performance in rugby. **8 marks**

Sample response extract

Rob's muscular system will have a greater number of mitochondria in his muscle cells. This is the site of aerobic respiration so his muscles will have more places for energy production, which increases the amount of energy that can be supplied aerobically so that Rob has the supply he needs to continue working to a good level all game.

Rob's myoglobin stores in his leg muscles increase, making oxygen more readily available to the muscle. This oxygen can be used in energy production, delaying the need to switch to anaerobic systems which could lead to muscle fatigue. Rob's muscles will increase their ability to store glycogen and triglycerides, providing further fuel sources for aerobic exercise, limiting the risk of fatigue during the game. These aerobic adaptations will also help Rob recover after high-intensity parts of the game as sufficient quantities of aerobic energy can be used to break down lactate reducing muscle fatigue.

Top tips

For a 6- or 8-mark question you need to:

☑ demonstrate accurate and thorough knowledge and understanding

☑ apply knowledge to the context of the question

☑ display a well-developed and logically balanced discussion or analysis, showing an awareness of competing arguments

☑ contain logical chains of reasoning throughout and the linkages between / within body systems

☑ use technical language consistently and fluently.

Links Go to pages 68–70 to revise principles of aerobic training.

The question says 'impact on energy production and performance'. Try to apply your knowledge of the adaptations to the impact on **rugby** performance. Make sure you focus on adaptations caused by training aerobically.

For this question you need to demonstrate a good understanding of aerobic adaptations to the muscular system and the aerobic energy system. You also need to show how this knowledge links to performance in a game such as rugby.

You could have also talked about capillarisation, or the use of rest days to allow recovery, avoiding overtraining or even injury. Clearly if injured, performance levels would drop.

Links Go to pages 38 and 39 to revise the content needed for this question.

Now try this

Becker is 35 years old and has high blood pressure. He is returning to physical activity after a ten-year gap and has joined a new gym.

Discuss the effects of participating in physical activity on the cardiovascular system for an individual suffering with high blood pressure.

 Links Go to pages 33–34 to revise this topic.

 'Discuss' means exploring more than one viewpoint.

Exercise and physical activity

It is widely proven that individuals who regularly partake in physical activity or exercise are less prone to significant health problems, ranging from obesity to many chronic diseases.

Physical and psychological benefits of exercise

Improves body shape · Reduces risk of chronic conditions · Weight control · Improves posture · Improves flexibility / balance

Alleviates anxiety · Relieves stress · Reduces depression

Health benefits of exercise

Strengthens bones · Boosts energy levels · Boosts immune system · Improves sleep

Improves mood / self-esteem · Improves concentration · Healthy growth / development

Social and economic benefits

Social:
- encourages social interaction
- improves social skills
- reduces isolation
- enhances self-esteem / confidence.

Economic:
- reduces NHS costs
- creates employment
- supports businesses
- reduces absenteeism in the workplace.

Key definitions

Physical activity is any activity that increases energy expenditure above resting level.

Exercise is physical activity with more structure and is usually undertaken for fitness gains.

Sedentary lifestyle is a type of lifestyle with no or irregular physical activity.

Remember, physical activity has to be current and continued for there to be health benefits.

Examples of physical activity/exercise

- Everyday activities – for example, walking / cycling to work / school, housework, gardening, DIY or any active / manual work as part of a job.
- Active recreational activities – for example, dancing, active play amongst children, or walking or cycling for recreation.
- Sport – for example, exercise and fitness training at a gym or during an exercise class, swimming and competitive sports such as football, rugby and tennis, etc.
- Positive risk-taking activities – for example, activities that promote endorphin release and improved confidence levels, such as rock climbing, sky diving, white water rafting, etc.

Physical activity/exercise: government recommendations

Children and young people (5–18 years)	Adults (19–64 years)	Older adults (65+ years)
• Moderate–vigorous physical activity for 60 min per day • Vigorous activities 3 times a week minimum • Activity for strength – 3 times a week	• Moderate activity 30 min – five times per week • Moderate / vigorous activity – 150 min spread across week • Activity for strength – 2 times a week	• Should be active daily • Moderate / vigorous activity – 150 min spread across week • Activity for strength – 2 times a week

Now try this

Jack is a 35-year-old office worker who plays 5-a side football for two 1-hour sessions per week.

(a) Compare Jack's current exercise to government recommendations.

(b) What would you recommend?

A balanced diet

An increasing number of adults and children are classified as overweight or obese. This simply means that many of us are eating more than we actually need.

What is a balanced diet?

- Eating the right amount of food to achieve / maintain a healthy body weight.
- Eating a wide variety of foods in the right proportions.

The Eat Well Plate shows the different types of food that should make up our diet, and the required proportions we should eat them in.

Benefits of a healthy diet

These include:

- improves immune function
- increases energy and vitality
- prevents disease and improves mood
- maintains a healthy weight
- reduced risk of developing chronic diseases.

The NHS key recommendations from the Eat Well Plate

The recommendations are to eat:

- plenty of fruit and vegetables
- plenty of potatoes, bread, rice and pasta
- some milk and dairy foods
- some meat, fish, eggs and beans
- a small amount of food / drink high in fat or sugar.

Fluid intake

Water is essential for life; it is very important to get the right amount of fluid to be healthy.

To maintain **water balance** a sedentary individual requires **2–2.5 litres** of fluid per day (6–8 glasses).

Physical activity, the weather and age determine how much fluid we require.

Moderation of caffeine intake

Caffeine is an addictive mild stimulant, which provides **no nutritional value**, so moderate caffeine consumption of around 400 mg (4–5 average cups) per day is recommended.

Remember we also get water from the food we eat; on average food provides about 20 per cent of our total fluid intake.

Strategies for improving dietary intake

☑ **Timing of meals** – eat at appropriate times to aid fat burning, reduce hunger and balance stress hormones. Breakfast is the most important meal of the day. Eating late at night can produce negative effects, such as sleep issues, weight gain, heart burn and acid reflux.

☑ **Number of meals** – you should aim to eat at regular intervals (every 3–4 hours).

☑ **Food choices** – ensure a balance of food groups; aim to eat five fruits / vegetables a day. Reduce salt intake. Aim to consume recommended calories (2500 men/2000 women). Check food labels for healthier options, such as those low in salt / sugar.

☑ **Drink alcohol in moderation** – as per government guidelines.

☑ **Consider portion sizes** – reduce sizes and avoid second helpings.

☑ **Food organisation and preparation** – plan meals the night before, consider how meals are cooked, such as grilling rather than frying.

☑ **Eat slower** – it takes the brain time to register.

Now try this

(a) Many clients don't have time for breakfast. Suggest **two** strategies to help them make time.

(b) Does drinking coffee and tea count towards our fluid intake?

Negative effects of smoking

Smoking increases your risk of developing more than 50 serious health conditions. Some are fatal while others can cause irreversible long-term damage to your health.

Smoking statistics

There are about **10 million adults** who smoke cigarettes in Great Britain: this is about $\frac{1}{6}$ of the total UK population.

In Great Britain, 22 per cent of adult men and 17 per cent of adult women are smokers.

Every year, around **100 000** smokers in the UK die from smoking related causes.

Smoking accounts for $\frac{1}{3}$ of respiratory deaths, over $\frac{1}{4}$ of cancer deaths, and about $\frac{1}{7}$ of cardiovascular disease deaths.

Smoking and cancer

Lung cancer is the most common form of cancer associated with smoking. It also causes cancer in many other parts of the body, including the:

- mouth
- lips
- throat
- voice box (larynx)
- oesophagus (the tube between your mouth and stomach)
- bladder
- kidney
- liver
- stomach
- pancreas.

The age at which you start smoking appears to be significant in the risk of developing lung cancer.

Smoking – heart-related conditions

Smoking damages your heart and your blood circulation, increasing your risk of developing conditions such as coronary heart disease, heart attack, stroke, peripheral vascular disease (damaged blood vessels) or cerebrovascular disease (damaged arteries that supply blood to your brain).

Smoking – lung-related conditions

Smoking also damages your lungs, leading to conditions such as chronic obstructive pulmonary disease (COPD), which incorporates bronchitis and emphysema/pneumonia.

Other health-related problems

Smoking can also:

- worsen/prolong the symptoms of respiratory conditions such as asthma, or respiratory tract infections such as the common cold
- cause infertility – male and female smokers are likely to have more fertility problems than non smokers.

Ten health benefits of stopping smoking

Stopping smoking provides the following benefits:

- ✓ breath more easily
- ✓ gives you more energy
- ✓ less stressed
- ✓ better sex life
- ✓ improves fertility
- ✓ improves smell and taste
- ✓ younger looking skin
- ✓ whiter teeth and fresher breath
- ✓ live longer
- ✓ protects your loved ones from second-hand smoke inhalation.

Now try this

Recall **three** of the negative effects of smoking.

Negative effects of alcohol

Drinking too much on a single occasion or over time can seriously affect health.

Key points

1 Alcohol is legal for those aged 18 and over. This doesn't mean it's any less powerful than other drugs.

2 Alcohol is a depressant, which means it slows down your body's responses in all kinds of ways.

3 Moderate consumption can make you feel sociable; too much and you'll have a hangover the next day.

4 Excessive consumption of alcohol in a single session could put you in a coma or even kill you.

Effects of alcohol on the body

Short-term effects include nausea, vomiting, blackouts, memory loss and anxiety.

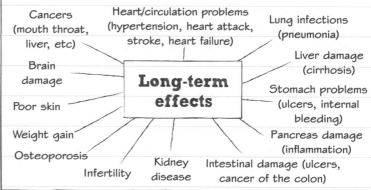

Long-term effects:
- Cancers (mouth throat, liver, etc)
- Heart/circulation problems (hypertension, heart attack, stroke, heart failure)
- Lung infections (pneumonia)
- Brain damage
- Liver damage (cirrhosis)
- Poor skin
- Stomach problems (ulcers, internal bleeding)
- Weight gain
- Pancreas damage (inflammation)
- Osteoporosis
- Infertility
- Kidney disease
- Intestinal damage (ulcers, cancer of the colon)

Mental health problems

Alcohol is sometimes used to help cope with difficult situations/emotions/reduce stress and relieve anxiety, but, in fact, alcohol can be associated with a range of mental health problems, including:

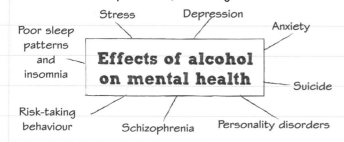

Effects of alcohol on mental health:
- Stress
- Depression
- Anxiety
- Poor sleep patterns and insomnia
- Suicide
- Risk-taking behaviour
- Schizophrenia
- Personality disorders

Empty calories

Alcohol is high in sugar, equalling **calories**.

These are 'empty calories' and have no nutritional value. The calories in alcohol are metabolised first by the body, ahead of burning fat, which is not desirable if on a weight loss programme.

Key term

Metabolism – the chemical processes that happen in the body to keep us alive and allow our organs to function normally, such as breathing, repairing cells and digesting food.

Government recommendations and guidelines

✓ Men and women are advised not to regularly drink more than **14 units** a week.

✓ **Spread your drinking** over three days or more if you drink as much as 14 units a week.

Examples of units in common drinks

9 units	2 units	2.1 units	1.5 units	1.7 units	1 unit
1 bottle (750 ml) of wine based on 13% ABV	1 pint of beer based on 3.6% ABV	1 medium (175 ml) glass of wine based on 12% ABV	1 bottle (275 ml) of alcopops based on 5.5% ABV	1 bottle (300 ml) of premium beer based on 5% ABV	1 glass of 25 ml measured spirits based on 40% ABV

The number of units in a drink is based on the size of the drink as well as its alcohol strength.

Now try this

Sam meets his friends four nights a week in his local pub, consuming approximately three pints of lager on each occasion. Compare Sam's alcohol intake to government recommendations.

Stress and sleep

Stress and a poor sleep pattern can interlink – affecting how we feel, think, behave and how our body works.

What is stress?

Stress is the feeling of being under too much mental or emotional pressure.

Pressure turns into stress when you feel unable to cope. People have different ways of reacting to stress, so a situation that feels stressful to one person may be motivating to someone else.

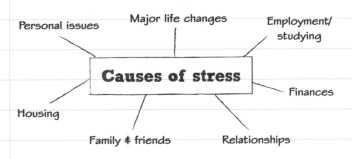

Personal issues

Major life changes

Employment/ studying

Causes of stress

Finances

Housing

Family & friends

Relationships

Some of the effects of stress

How you might feel	How you might behave	How you might be physically affected
Irritable	Find it hard to make decisions	Problems sleeping / staying asleep
Anxious / nervous	Poor concentration	Tired all the time
Depressed	Eating too much / too little	Headaches
Lonely	Tearful / crying	Constipation / diarrhoea
Can't switch off	Smoking / drinking more than usual	Feeling sick / dizzy / faint

Long-term effects of stress

These include:

- poor immune system
- skin conditions
- heart disease / heart attack
- stroke
- hypertension
- angina
- stomach ulcers
- depression.

Role of sleep

Sleep is a restorative state which plays a vital role in our health. If sleep is cut short, the body doesn't have time to complete all the phases needed for:

- muscle repair
- memory consolidation
- release of hormones regulating growth and appetite.

Effects of poor sleep

Poor immune system

Heart disease

Diabetes

Poor mental health

Cold and flu

Effects of poor sleep on health

Reduced sex drive

Memory problems

Infertility problems

Stroke

High blood pressure

Stress

Recommendations

The NHS recommends that we need approximately **8 hours** of good-quality sleep a night to function properly. Some individuals need more or less.

Sleep requirements vary with age.

Now try this

Paul is stressed on a daily basis because he has a demanding workload; he only allows himself an average of 6 hours sleep per night.

(a) Compare this to the NHS recommendations for sleep.

(b) How might his sleep pattern cause him additional stress?

Barriers to change

Different barriers may present themselves in tackling health behaviours; particularly individuals embarking on physical activity. Strategies are essential to overcome these barriers.

Barriers to exercise

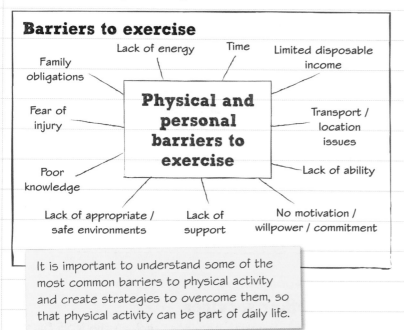

It is important to understand some of the most common barriers to physical activity and create strategies to overcome them, so that physical activity can be part of daily life.

Overcoming the time barrier

'I don't have **time** to exercise'.

- Prioritise and manage your daily routine / schedule; identify available time slots.
- Incorporate exercise into your daily routine, such as when travelling to and from work.
- Adapt what you do at work; for example, exercise in your lunch hour, use the stairs instead of the lift, stand up while making phone calls, have walking meetings.
- Adapt leisure time activities; undertake a new activity.
- Select activities that require minimal time.

Overcoming the cost barrier

'I can't **afford** a gym membership.'

- Walking to work or increasing activity at home (gardening, housework) is free.
- Walking and jogging are low in cost.
- Exercise at home – press ups, squats, workout DVDs.

Overcoming the transport/location barrier

'The gym is **too far** from my house.'

- Less reliance on the car increases activity levels.
- Consider your location and how it can be used to maximum benefit. If it's local, walk.
- When commuting, get off one stop earlier and walk the remaining distance.
- Park your car further away and walk.

Overcoming lack of energy/ motivation

'I don't have the **energy**, I can't be **bothered**.'

- Schedule exercise when you have most energy or plan ahead.
- Think positively: exercise will increase your energy levels.
- Invite a friend.
- Exercise in the morning to avoid excuses.
- Ensure a variety of activities.
- Set achievable goals.

Overcoming family obligations as a barrier

'I don't have time to exercise because of the **children**.'

- Trade babysitting with a friend, neighbour or family member.
- Exercise with the kids or when they are not around.
- Get a bike or use home gymnasium equipment.

Now try this

Consider **two** strategies you would employ if your client says 'Exercise is boring'.

Smoking cessation strategies

Giving up smoking is probably the biggest single step we can take to improve our health. However, this can prove to be challenging, as nicotine is a powerful and addictive substance.

Ten self-help tips

Making small lifestyle changes may help when quitting smoking:

1. thinking positively
2. making a plan to quit
3. dietary changes
4. drinking changes
5. identifying the times when we crave cigarettes
6. getting some stop–smoking support
7. getting moving
8. making non-smoking friends
9. keeping the hands and mouth busy
10. making a list of reasons to quit.

Advantages and disadvantages of acupuncture

Acupuncture is a treatment derived from ancient Chinese medicine in which fine needles are inserted at certain sites in the body for therapeutic or preventative purposes.

👍 Stimulates the release of natural painkilling substances: endorphins

👍 Effective for some individuals

👎 Limited scientific evidence to support effectiveness

👎 Costly.

Smoking helplines

Smoking helplines such as the NHS Smoking Helpline may be available for free.

 Links Go to page 46 to revise the effects of smoking.

Other services

Stop-smoking services, such as the NHS Smoking Services may also be available for free. It is worthwhile speaking with a GP to find out the services available.

Quit kit support packs – these contain free useful tools to help support quitting smoking.

Nicotine replacement therapy (NRT)

NRT works by steadily releasing nicotine into the bloodstream at lower levels than in a cigarette, without the tar, carbon monoxide and other poisonous chemicals present in tobacco smoke, helping to control cravings.

Skin patches　　Chewing gum

Mouth spray —　**Forms of NRT**　— Inhalators

Nasal spray　　Tablets / strips / lozenges

There is no evidence that one type of NRT is more effective. Choice is down to personal preference.

Side effects of NRT

Side effects can include skin irritation (patches), irritation of nose, throat or eyes (nasal spray), disturbed sleep, vivid dreams, upset stomach, dizziness or headaches.

Which form of NRT?

For example:

☑ heavy smokers may use 24-hour patches

☑ nasal/mouth sprays are the fastest acting form of NRT

☑ some find it useful to combine NRT products.

NRT usually lasts 8–12 weeks before reduction of the dose and eventually stopping.

Now try this

Quitting smoking and weight gain are often linked. What advice would you give to a client who shows concern over this?

Reducing alcohol consumption

To cut down on alcohol successfully, easy-to-adopt steps can be put into practice.

Aiming to drink less

✓ Break habits and do something different at the time of day when drinking occurs.

✓ Have at least two days a week without drinking.

✓ Pace drinking; sipping slowly and enjoying the taste.

✓ Space out drinks; have a soft drink/water in between.

✓ Have a smaller drink; a single instead of a double.

✓ Choose a drink with less alcohol.

Reducing alcohol consumption at home

Keep track · Drink with food · Only have one with your meal · Distract yourself · **Tips to reduce drinking at home** · Use a drinks measure · Avoid stocking up · Don't leave the bottle on the table

Reducing drinking while out

- Meet somewhere that doesn't serve alcohol.
- Set a limit, or opt out of rounds.
- Budget: take out a fixed amount of money to spend on alcohol.
- Go out later.
- Sit down – we drink more slowly when sitting down compared to standing.

Self-help groups

- **Drinkline** is the national alcohol helpline.
- **Alcoholics Anonymous (AA)** is a free self-help group. Its 12-step programme involves getting sober with the help of regular support groups.
- **Al-Anon Family Groups** offer support and understanding to the families/friends of problem drinkers.

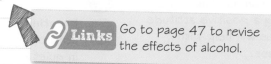

Links Go to page 47 to revise the effects of alcohol.

Counselling

Specially trained therapists may offer counselling to individuals/groups. **Cognitive behavioural therapy (CBT)** is one of the most effective forms.

- It tackles patterns of thinking / behaviour, to break certain emotional / psychological ties to habits.
- It addresses the underlying feelings and thought processes causing addiction.
- It helps find ways to address problems / insecurities, without turning to alcohol.

Alternative treatments

Individuals trying to overcome alcohol problems may choose other treatments to boost chances for success.

Meditation · Yoga · Exercise · **Alternative treatments** · Acupuncture · Hypnotherapy · Nutritional counselling

There are mixed views on the effectiveness of alternative treatments.

Now try this

Suggest **two** strategies / tips you would give a client who drinks more than the recommended units of alcohol per week.

Managing stress

Some people cope with stress more effectively or recover from stressful events quicker than others. Stress management techniques are helpful for all.

Stress management techniques

Assertiveness training   Goal setting

Changes to work-life balance   **Stress management techniques**   Time management

Alternative therapies   Physical activity

Meditation   Breathing techniques   Relaxation   Positive self-talk

Good time management and prioritisation of workload and commitments are key to managing stress.

Assertiveness and goal-setting

- **Assertiveness** – means being confident enough to clearly and effectively express your feelings/opinions, while still valuing those of others. It impacts directly on the way that you communicate and interact with other people and helps build your self-esteem. Training in body language, communication, or receiving counselling or psychotherapy can develop assertiveness.

- **Goal setting** – setting achievable goals can motivate and reward, thus building self-confidence and reducing stress.

Physical activity and positive self-talk

- **Physical activity** – is effective in improving anxiety, depression, self-esteem and mood. It releases 'feel good hormones': endorphins. It also acts as a distractor from the stressor.

- **Positive self-talk** – is the inner dialogue you have with yourself. It involves taking an optimistic view of life and situations, such as challenges/difficulties/deadlines. Having a positive attitude and ways to deal with stress will help with managing and reducing stress.

Relaxation techniques

Relaxation ensures the body is relaxed and calm, resulting in decreasing heart rate, breathing rate, blood pressure and relaxing the muscles. Different techniques work for different individuals.

Two popular techniques are:

 meditation

 breathing techniques – focusing on controlling inhalation and exhalation, usually in quiet surroundings.

Alternative therapies and work-life balance

- **Alternative therapies** – these include acupuncture, herbal remedies and yoga. They often work well alongside other techniques.

- **Changes to work-life balance** – incorporating strategies at work to help alleviate stress such as regular breaks, not taking work home, informing employers if stressed, using relaxation techniques after work or engaging in leisure activities.

🔗 **Links** Go to page 48 to revise the effects of stress on sleep.

Tips to improve sleep

- ✓ Follow a regular bedtime routine.
- ✓ Avoid drinking coffee and tea.
- ✓ Take exercise during the day/avoid exercise two hours before bed.
- ✓ Ensure sleeping environment is comfortable.
- ✓ Avoid a heavy meal two hours before bed.
- ✓ Avoid using alcohol to help you sleep.
- ✓ Keep a to-do list beside the bed.
- ✓ Have a warm bath.
- ✓ Listen to relaxing music.
- ✓ Try breathing techniques.

Now try this

Joanne has a demanding workload and is stressed on a daily basis. She has never utilised stress management techniques before.

Justify how physical activity can be used to help Joanne alleviate her stress.

Screening processes

In a sport or fitness setting, it is imperative that you collect individual information from clients to provide the most appropriate advice and effectively tailor training programmes.

Screening consultations

You are likely to gather information to assess the lifestyle of an individual through a one-to-one consultation. During this, documentation, such as a questionnaire, will be completed which assesses lifestyle behaviours. Accurate screening can lead to overall production of a more effective training programme.

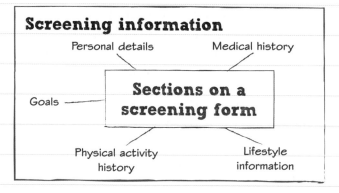

Screening information

Sections on a screening form

Personal details — Medical history — Goals — Physical activity history — Lifestyle information

Lifestyle questionnaires

Assessing a client's health status prior to embarking on a physical activity programme is an essential process. It provides an evaluation of the individual's current exercise, health and lifestyle; establishing their strengths and areas of improvement. It allows for the planning of realistic goals and injury avoidance.

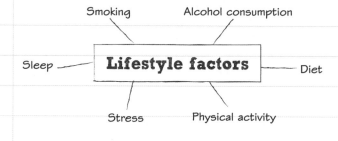

Lifestyle factors

Smoking — Alcohol consumption — Sleep — Diet — Stress — Physical activity

PAR-Q (Physical Activity Readiness Questionnaire)

A PAR-Q is a questionnaire used to assess a client's medical history. It determines the safety or possible risks based upon the individual answers given. There are about between 8 and 12 questions, which require a simple yes or no response.

For example:

> Do you ever feel pain in your chest when doing physical activity?
> Yes ☐   No ☐

If a client answers yes to a PAR-Q question, it is sensible to encourage them to seek clearance from their GP before beginning exercise.

Legal considerations

Screening clients accurately is important for insurance purposes; especially if you are a self-employed fitness instructor/personal trainer.

Key points to remember – client confidentiality

Information belongs to the client. It is privileged and subject to the Data Protection Act. This means that personal information should be stored securely and should be inaccessible by other people. Information should not be shared with a third party without the client's consent.

Data Protection Act – controls how personal information is used by an organisation, business or the government.

Informed consent – documented legal evidence that shows that participants have been provided with all the necessary information to undertake the exercise/fitness testing.

> ## Now try this
>
> (a) Give **two** advantages of the screening process.
> (b) Give **two** disadvantages of the screening process.

Blood pressure

Blood pressure (BP) measures the strain on the arteries and heart caused by the blood pushing against the sides of the blood vessels. It is a key indicator of an individual's current health status.

Blood pressure readings

Blood pressure is measured in 'millimetres of mercury' (mmHg) and is written as **two numbers**.

The first (or top) number is your **systolic** blood pressure. It is the highest level your blood pressure reaches when your heart beats.

The second (or bottom) number is your **diastolic** blood pressure. It is the lowest level your blood pressure reaches as your heart relaxes between beats.

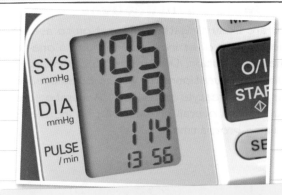

This person has a blood pressure reading of 105/69 mmHg, described as '105 over 69'.

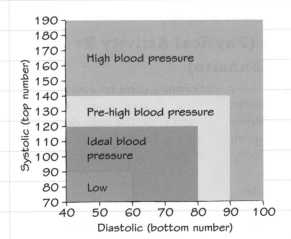

Normative data for BP

Interpreting blood pressure readings

Only one of the numbers has to be higher or lower to constitute as high/low blood pressure.

✓ **If the top number is 140 or more** – this may indicate high blood pressure, regardless of the bottom number.

✓ **If the bottom number is 90 or more** – this may indicate high blood pressure, regardless of the top number.

✓ **If the top number is 90 or less** – this may indicate low blood pressure, regardless of the bottom number.

✓ **If the bottom number is 60 or less** – this may indicate low blood pressure, regardless of the top number.

High blood pressure

High blood pressure is a significant health risk. It can cause:

- strain on heart and blood vessels
- increased risk of a heart attack
- increased risk of stroke
- kidney disease
- vascular dementia.

Treatment and prevention

Here are some ways to reduce high blood pressure:

✓ Eat less salt

✓ Eat more fruit and vegetables

✓ Maintain a healthy weight

✓ Drink less alcohol and stop smoking

✓ Get more active

✓ Reduce intake of coffee, tea, other caffeine-rich drinks.

Now try this

Your next client's blood pressure measures $\frac{138}{86}$ mmHg.

(a) Interpret this reading against normative data.

(b) Identify the areas on the screening form you would refer to to make initial recommendations.

Resting heart rate (RHR)

Resting heart rate can vary with fitness level and age – the fitter you are, generally the lower the resting heart rate.

Heart rate (HR)

Your heart rate is the number of times your heart **beats per minute.** The heart, like any other muscle, needs physical activity to keep it in good condition.

An adult's **normal resting heart rate** can range anywhere from 60 to 100 beats per minute (bpm), whilst resting. It will vary depending on: **when** it is measured and the **level of activity immediately before the reading.**

Factors affecting heart rate

- **Caffeine and alcohol** – increases the strength and frequency of the heartbeat.
- **Exercise** increases the HR, but someone who exercises regularly may have a lower resting rate.
- **Disease** affects the HR, for instance, thyroid disease can either make the rate faster or slower.
- **Drugs** (medical and recreational), such as beta blockers, slow the HR. Recreational drugs tend to increase HR.

Normative data for resting heart rate (RHR) – men

Age	18–25	26–35	36–45	46–55	56–65	65+
Athlete	49–55	49–54	50–56	50–57	51–56	50–55
Excellent	56–61	55–61	57–62	58–63	57–61	56–61
Good	62–65	62–65	63–66	64–67	62–67	62–65
Above average	66–69	66–70	67–70	68–71	68–71	66–69
Average	70–73	71–74	71–75	72–76	72–75	70–73
Below average	74–81	75–81	76–82	77–83	76–81	74–79
Poor	82+	82+	83+	84+	82+	80+

Normative data for resting heart rate (RHR) – women

Age	18–25	26–35	36–45	46–55	56–65	65+
Athlete	54–60	54–59	54–59	54–60	54–59	54–59
Excellent	61–65	60–64	60–64	61–65	60–64	60–64
Good	66–69	65–68	65–69	66–69	65–68	65–68
Above average	70–73	69–72	70–73	70–73	69–73	69–72
Average	74–78	73–76	74–78	74–77	74–77	73–76
Below average	79–84	77–82	79–84	78–83	78–83	77–84
Poor	85+	83+	85+	84+	84+	84+

Now try this

Your client, Chris, is 31 years old and his resting heart rate is 85 bpm.

(a) Interpret this reading against normative data.

(b) Identify the areas on the screening form you would refer to, to make initial recommendations to improve your client's resting heart rate.

Body mass index (BMI)

BMI is a measure that adults can use to see if they are a healthy weight for their height. Research shows a significant relationship between high BMI and cardiovascular disease and diabetes.

How to calculate BMI

$$BMI = \frac{Weight\ (kg)}{Height\ (m)} = \frac{Total}{Height\ (m)}$$

Worked example

Gina measures 1.6 metres tall and weighs 70 kilograms.

$$BMI = \frac{70}{1.6} = \frac{43.75}{1.6} = 27.34 = 27\ kg/m^2$$

Acceptable BMI

- Less than 18.5 = underweight
- **Between 18.5 to 24.9 = healthy weight**
- 25–29.9 = overweight
- 30–39.9 = obese
- 40 or more is very obese

These ranges are only for adults. BMI is interpreted differently for children.

High BMI / Overweight

If BMI is 25 or above, you weigh more than is ideal for your height.

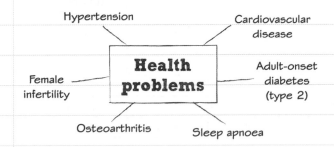

BMI can mean an increased risk of developing some of the above health problems.

Low BMI / Underweight

If BMI is less than 18.5, you weigh less than is ideal for your height.

Low BMI can mean an increased risk of developing health problems, such as:

- brittle bones (osteoporosis)
- absent periods in women (amenorrhoea)
- iron deficiency (anaemia).

Accuracy of BMI

As BMI is based on the height and weight of a person, it is an **inaccurate** measure of body fat content.

It does not take into account muscle mass, bone density, or overall body composition. It doesn't take into account where a person carries his/her body fat, or racial and gender differences.

Strategies to lower BMI

These include:

- healthy eating/balanced diet
- increasing activity
- drinking more fluids.

Muscle is much denser than fat so very muscular people, such as heavyweight boxers, may be a healthy weight even though their BMI is classed as obese.

Now try this

James measures 1.75 m tall and weighs 85 kg.

(a) Calculate his BMI.

(b) Give **two** considerations you would need to take into account about James' BMI before making any recommendations.

Waist-to-hip ratio

Fat distribution, as measured by the **waist-to-hip ratio (WHR)**, has been found to identify those at risk of health complications.

Measuring the waist-to-hip ratio

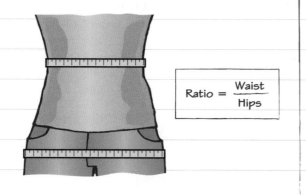

$$\text{Ratio} = \frac{\text{Waist}}{\text{Hips}}$$

Conducting the test

To calculate waist-to-hip ratio:

1 Measure the hips – **maximum circumference of buttocks.**

2 Measure the waist – **narrowest part of the torso.**

3 Divide the waist number by the hip number.

Obesity definitions

There are three forms of obesity.

1 **Peripheral obesity** is the accumulation of excess fat in the buttocks, hips and thighs.

2 **Central obesity** is an excess accumulation of fat in the abdominal area.

3 A combination of peripheral and central obesity.

Normative data for the waist-to-hip ratio

hip ratio Male	Female	Related health risks
0.95 or below	0.80 or below	Low risk
0.96 to 1.0	0.81 to 0.85	Moderate risk
1.0+	0.85+	High risk

Acceptable waist-to-hip readings

A ratio of 1.0 or more in men or 0.85 or more in women indicates carrying too much weight around the middle. **Excessive weight around the waist increases the risk for certain diseases, compared to carrying more weight around the hips.**

Advantages and disadvantages of the waist-to-hip ratio

👍 Quick risk factor assessment

👍 Can be completed at home

👍 Only requires a tape measure

👍 Can be used to determine changes in body composition over time.

👎 Does not take into account lean body mass

👎 Does not take into account fat mass

👎 Open to human error when measuring

Now try this

Rob's waist measures 39 inches and his hips measure 37 inches.

(a) Calculate his waist-to-hip measurement.

(b) Interpret the measurement against normative data.

(c) Based on his WHR measurements only, provide **two** recommendations for Rob.

Nutritional terminology

Nutrition is about eating a healthy and balanced diet. Understanding nutritional terminology may make it easier to make better food choices.

Food labelling

Nutritional labels include information on:

1. Energy: **8400 kJ / 2000 kcal**
2. Total fat: **70 g**
3. Saturates: **20 g**
4. Carbohydrate: **260 g**
5. Total sugars: **90 g**
6. Protein: **50 g**
7. Salt: **6 g**

The bold figures above represent an adult's reference intake (RI) for a day.

Key point: Nutrition information is provided per 100 g and sometimes per portion of the food.

Recommended daily allowance (RDAs) or Daily reference intakes (RIs)

These are guidelines about the approximate amount of particular nutrients / calories required for a healthy diet. Requirements for calories / nutrients are different for all individuals. **RDAs are not intended as targets** but as a useful indication of how a particular nutrient or amount of energy fits into the daily diet.

SERVES 1 – THIS PACK PROVIDES				
CALS	SUGAR	FAT	SAT FAT	SALT
315	3.6 g	12.6 g	8.1 g	1.80 g
16%	4%	18%	41%	30%
OF YOUR GUIDELINE DAILY AMOUNT				

The RDAs are shown as a percentage

Other food measures include **calories** and **joules (international system)** which are a measure of the amount of energy in food:

✓ 1000 calories = 1 **kilocalorie** = 1 kcal

✓ 1000 joules = 1 **kilojoule** = 1 kJ.

Estimated average requirements (EAR)

Energy intake is compared against the estimated average requirement (EAR) for a group. Estimates of energy requirements for different populations are defined as the energy intake estimated to meet the average (median) requirements of the group. About half the people in the group will need more energy than the EAR and half the people in the group will need less.

Colour coding

The colour coding used on some nutritional labels, at a glance, tells us if the food is high, medium or low in calories, sugar, fat, saturated fat and salt.

RED = high in this nutrient, these foods need to be eaten less often and in small amounts.

AMBER = medium in this nutrient, these foods/ drinks can be eaten most of the time.

GREEN = low in this nutrient, the healthier choice.

Lower reference nutrient intake (LRNI)

This is the amount of a nutrient that is sufficient for only a few members of the group who have exceptionally low requirements. Intakes below the LRNI by most individuals within the group will almost certainly be inadequate.

Safe intake (SI)

This is the range used where there is insufficient evidence to set an EAR, RNI or LRNI. The safe intake is the amount judged to be enough for almost everyone, but below a level that could have undesirable effects. The amount of each nutrient needed differs. Individual requirements of each nutrient are related to a person's age, gender, level of physical activity and health status.

Now try this

(a) Compare this product against RDAs.

(b) Using the colour coding, is this product a healthy choice?

This pack provides:				
Cal	Fat	Saturates	Sugar	Salt
218	12 g	6 g	0.7 g	0.6 g
(11%)	(19%)	(30%)	(<1%)	(12%)

Energy balance

Understanding how many calories are in our food can help us to balance the energy we put into our bodies with the energy we use. This is key to maintaining a healthy weight.

What is energy balance?

 Weight gain/positive energy balance occurs when we regularly put more energy into our bodies than we use. Over time, that excess energy is stored by the body as fat.

 Weight loss/negative energy balance occurs when we don't put enough energy into the body for what we use.

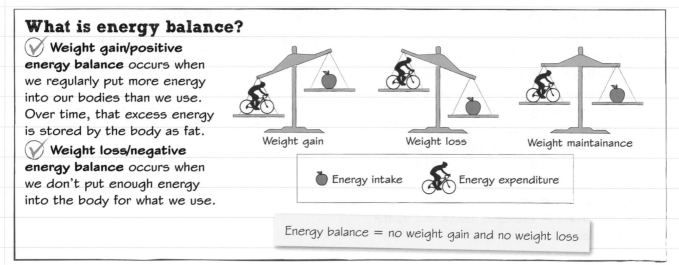

Weight gain   Weight loss   Weight maintainance

🍎 Energy intake   🚴 Energy expenditure

Energy balance = no weight gain and no weight loss

Components of energy output

1 **Resting metabolic rate (RMR)**

The number of calories your body burns if you do nothing. The energy used to keep the essential body functions going. It accounts for 60–75 per cent of total energy expenditure.

2 **Dietary thermogenesis (DT)**

Refers to the energy expended above that of RMR for the processes of digestion, absorption, transport and storage of food. It is influenced by calories content and composition of diet along with individual nutritional status.

3 **Physical activity (PA)**

Represents the most variable component of your total energy expenditure (energy above RMR and DT). Exactly how much it varies depends on how active your lifestyle is (frequency, intensity, time and type).

4 **Adaptive thermogenesis**

This is energy expenditure that occurs as a result of environmental or physiological stresses placed on your body, such as a change in temperature which requires a response of shivering or stress that causes anxiety and fidgeting.

Basal metabolic rate (BMR)

This is the number of calories expended to maintain essential processes, such as breathing and organ function during sleep.

BMR is affected by a number of factors:

- **Age** – BMR **decreases** with increasing age.
- **Gender** – males generally have a **higher** BMR due to greater muscle mass.
- **Climate** – exposure to hot/cold climates causes an **increase** in BMR.
- **Physical activity** – affects the energy requirements needed.
- **Moderate-intensity activities:** walking, golfing and yoga – between 150 and 300 calories per hour.
- **High-intensity activities:** basketball, running and swimming – approximately 500 calories plus per hour.

Now try this

(a) Explain how weight gain occurs.

(b) Explain how weight loss occurs.

Macronutrients

Carbohydrates, protein and fats are classed as macronutrients as they are required in large amounts on a daily basis. These are the nutrients that provide energy within our diet.

Carbohydrates

Carbohydrates:

- are the body's main sources of fuel
- are easily used by the body for energy
- all carbohydrates consumed end up as glucose to provide energy
- are needed for the central nervous system, the kidneys, the brain and the muscles (including the heart) to function properly
- can be stored in the muscles and liver and later used for energy
- are important in intestinal health and waste elimination.

Types of carbohydrates

Simple	Complex
'Quick release energy'	'Slow release energy'
Sugar, jam, fizzy drinks	Bread, bagels, rice, pasta, cereals

Complex carbohydrates should comprise **50–60 per cent** of total calories consumed. More active individuals will need 70 per cent to replace depleted glycogen store.

Protein

Protein should comprise **12–20** per cent of our total calories. We need this protein for:

- growth (important for children/teens/pregnant women)
- building and repairing tissue
- immunity function
- making essential hormones/enzymes
- energy when carbohydrates are not available
- preserving lean muscle mass.

Types of protein

Complete proteins	Incomplete proteins
Meat, poultry, fish, milk, cheese	Cereals, bread, rice, pasta, beans

On average:

- men should consume no more than **55 g** a day
- women should consume no more than **45 g** per day.

Fats

Fats should comprise **20–35** per cent of our total calories. We need fat for:

- normal growth and development
- energy (fat is the most concentrated source of energy)
- absorbing certain vitamins (like vitamins A, D, E, K)
- providing heat insulation, cushioning and buoyancy for the organs
- maintaining cell membranes
- providing taste, consistency, and stability to foods.

Types of fats

Saturated	Monosaturated	Polyunsaturated
Butter, meat, lard, cream	Olive oil, rapeseed oil, peanut butter	Soft margarine, low-fat spreads, soya oil

Too much saturated fat within our diet causes significant health problems. The government recommends that:

- men should consume no more than **30 g** a day
- women should consume no more than **20 g** per day.

Now try this

Explain the reasoning behind endurance athletes reducing fat intake and consuming more carbohydrates.

Vitamins A, B and C

Micronutrients are dietary components, often referred to as vitamins and minerals, which although only required by the body in small amounts, are vital to development, disease prevention, and well-being.

Vitamin A

Vitamin A:

- is a fat-soluble vitamin
- is needed for the normal functioning of the eyes and respiratory tract
- keeps the immune system healthy
- has two forms:

Retinol (animal sources)	Carotenoids (plant sources)
Liver, whole milk	Green leafy vegetables, carrots and orange coloured fruits

Too much or too little vitamin A?

Adults need: 0.7 mg a day for men/0.6 mg a day for women.

Too much vitamin A causes an increased risk of fractures.

Consuming too much whilst pregnant has also been linked to birth defects.

Deficiency leads to poor vision/ blindness.

A good source of vitamin A

Vitamin B

All B vitamins have important functions.

- They support the breakdown and release of energy from food.
- They keep the eyes, skin and nervous system healthy.
- Examples of sources are: lean meats, eggs, cereal and wholegrain breads.

Too much or too little vitamin B?

There is limited evidence of the issues caused by too much vitamin B.

Most vitamins cannot be produced by your body and must be supplied by a balanced diet.

A good source of vitamin B

Vitamin C

Vitamin C:

- is also known as ascorbic acid
- helps to protect cells, keeps them healthy
- is needed in maintenance of healthy connective tissue
- helps wound healing
- acts as an antioxidant that protects the body from damage by free radicals.

Vitamin C
Fresh citrus fruits and berries, green vegetables, peppers and tomatoes

Too much or too little vitamin C?

Adults need 40 mg of vitamin C a day.

- Scurvy can result from lack of ascorbic acid. Scurvy leads to spots on the skin, bleeding gums and loose or loss of teeth.
- Overnutrition of ascorbic acid is rare.

A good source of vitamin C

Now try this

Give **two** examples of food sources for the following vitamins:

(a) Vitamin A

(b) Vitamin B

(c) Vitamin C.

Vitamin D, calcium and iron

Micronutrients are essential food factors required in only small quantities.

Vitamin D

Vitamin D:

- is needed for the absorption of calcium and phosphorous from foods, keeping bones healthy
- enhances immune function and improves muscle strength
- found in our diet, but most is gained from sunlight.

Good sources of vitamin D

Too much or too little vitamin D?

- Too much can lead to excess levels of calcium in the blood.
- Deficiency of vitamin D leads to rickets and the formation of soft bones.
- Deficiency in adults can cause pain and muscular weakness.

Young children, housebound older adults and people practising certain religions where their skin must be covered are at risk of deficiency through lack of exposure of their skin to sunlight.

Calcium

Calcium is used for:

- helping to build strong bones and teeth
- regulating muscle contractions, including heartbeat
- ensuring that blood clots normally
- sources include milk, cheese and other dairy foods, and green leafy vegetables.

Good sources of calcium

Too much or too little calcium?

Adults need 700 mg of calcium a day.

- Taking high doses of calcium supplements can cause stomach pains and diarrhoea.
- Poor intakes of calcium can result in poor bone health, which can increase the risk of diseases such as osteoporosis later in life.

Iron

Iron:

- is needed for the formation of haemoglobin in red blood cells, which transport oxygen around the body
- is also required for energy metabolism and has an important role in the immune system
- sources include liver, meat, beans, nuts and dried fruit such as dried apricots.

A good source of iron

Too much or too little iron?

Adults need: 8.7 mg a day for men / 14.8 mg a day for women.

- Too much iron in the diet can result in constipation, nausea and vomiting.
- A lack of iron will lead to anaemia.

Now try this

Do athletes need to take extra supplements of vitamins and minerals?

Hydration and dehydration

Understanding the relationship between hydration and sports performance is vital for achieving optimal performance in training and competition.

Hydration

- Vital for transporting nutrients, waste products and internal secretions.
- Vital for temperature regulation.
- Aids the passage of food through the digestive system.
- Water makes up 45–65 per cent of total body weight.
- Muscle has a higher water content than fat tissue.
- Water is lost through several routes: urine / faeces / evaporation (skin) and expired breath.

Effects on fluid amounts

Climate – a hot/humid climate will require an increase in fluid intake.

Levels of exercise – athletes need to ensure they are fully hydrated before exercise, during and after.

Programme type – the more intense the activity, the more absorption is slowed down.

Time of year – more care to maintain hydration levels is needed in the summer months.

High water loss causes the body to dehydrate. Adequate fluid intake is crucial for an athlete.

Dehydration

Dehydration can impair athletes' **strength, power and aerobic capacity.** Severe dehydration can be fatal.

Just a 2 per cent loss of water can affect ability.

Signs and symptoms of dehydration include: lack of energy, early fatigue in exercise, feeling hot, clammy / flushed skin, nausea, not needing to go to the toilet, **headache, disorientation or shortness of breath.**

Those in bold are signs of advanced dehydration.

Hyperhydration

Hyperhydration is a state of excessive hydration, producing greater than normal body water content.

Starting exercise in this state can improve:

- thermoregulation
- heat dissipation
- exercise performance.

The symptoms of hyperhydration often mimic those of dehydration.

Fluid intake when exercising

- **Pre-event:** 300–500 ml of fluid 10–15 minutes before exercise.
- **Inter-event:** 150–200 ml every 15–20 minutes during exercise, especially if the exercise lasts longer than an hour.
- **Post event:** after exercise fluid losses should be replaced 1.5 times within the first 2 hours of recovery.

Training should be used to practise fluid replacement strategies.

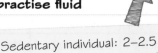

Sedentary individual: 2–2.5 litres per day / 6–8 cups of fluid

Fluid sources / requirements

Water – is adequate and suitable for most exercise. **Sports drinks** – are useful if exercising at higher intensities and for longer durations.

Ten per cent of daily requirements come from metabolic processes which release water from the body. **Ninety per cent is taken from the diet.**

Now try this

Why is it important for athletes to practise their fluid replacement strategies during training?

Nutritional strategies

The purpose of nutritional strategies in sport is to enhance training and performance.

Adapting diet to gain weight

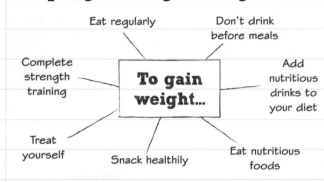

Eat regularly · Don't drink before meals · Complete strength training · Add nutritious drinks to your diet · Treat yourself · Snack healthily · Eat nutritious foods

To gain weight...

Adapting diet to lose weight

Don't skip breakfast · Eat regular meals · Plan meals · Eat plenty of fruit / veg · Reduce alcohol · Get more active · Drink plenty of water · Don't stock junk food · Don't ban food groups · Use a smaller plate · Read food labels · Eat high-fibre foods

To lose weight...

Ergogenic aids

Ergogenic aids are used to improve performance during high-intensity physical exercise. They give you a mental or physical edge while exercising or competing.

Energy gels / bars:

- help replenish carbohydrates
- help replenish glycogen/calories
- deliver a quick supply of energy to your muscles when you need it most – on the go
- are light and easily digestible
- can be consumed on the move.

The timing and frequency of using energy gels / bars is crucial for effectiveness.

Protein supplements

Powders are the most popular and are generally consumed immediately before and after exercising, or in place of a meal. They are used to:

👍 increase muscle size and strength
👍 reduce muscle soreness post-training
👍 accelerate gains in aerobic strength
👍 accelerate gains in anaerobic strength
👍 increase fat loss
👍 reduce hunger.

Problems with protein supplements:

👎 excess calories and protein intake
👎 taste
👎 cost

Carbohydrate loading

- A strategy to increase the amount of fuel stored in your muscles to improve athletic performance for endurance events
- Involves continuing to eat a high-carbohydrate 'training diet' while scaling back your activity level
- Carb-loading is most beneficial for endurance athletes, such as marathon runners, swimmers or cyclists
- Carb-loading is completed the week prior to high-endurance activity.

Sports drinks

Sports drinks aim to provide three nutrients:

carbohydrates – replace energy

water – replace fluid

electrolytes – replace minerals lost sweating.

Three types of sports drinks

	Hypotonic	Isotonic	Hypertonic
Carb content	1–3%	6–8%	10%+
Purpose	Quickly replace fluid lost	Quickly replace fluid lost & boost carbs	To supplement carb intake
Used by	Gymnasts, jockeys	Athletes, footballers	Athletes needing high energy, marathon runners

Now try this

Do power athletes need more protein in their diet than an endurance athlete?

Aerobic strength and muscular endurance

Physical fitness is related to overall health. The more physically fit an individual is, the less chance there is of developing health issues.

Aerobic endurance

This is the ability of the heart (cardiovascular system) and lungs (respiratory system) to supply the exercising muscles with oxygen to maintain the exercise for a long period of time.

Can also be known as cardiorespiratory endurance.

By maintaining the flow of oxygen, an individual is able to exercise continuously for longer periods of time without tiring.

Sporting relevance

Aerobic endurance is one of the **main fitness components**, important for success in many sports. Within certain sports it is the most important attribute, whereas in other sports it is only part of the overall fitness profile.

Key attribute	Part of the overall profile
Distance running, cycling, swimming or rowing	Racket sports
Triathlon	Team sports: football, netball, basketball or rugby

Strength

This is the ability of a specific muscle or muscle group to exert a force in a single maximal contraction against a resistance.

The Olympic rings is predominantly performed by male gymnasts due to its extreme upper body strength requirements.

Sporting relevance

Key attribute	Part of the overall profile
Weight lifting	Rugby
Wrestling	Gymnastics

Muscular endurance

This is the ability of a specific muscle or muscle group to sustain repeated contractions over an extended period of time.

Sporting relevance

Key attribute	Part of the overall profile
Distance running, cycling, swimming or rowing	Racket sports
Triathlon	Team sports: football, netball, basketball or rugby

Now try this

Justify how the component 'muscular endurance' is one of the main attributes required by a triathlete.

Flexibility, speed and body composition

Physical fitness is made up of a number of different components, each contributing to an individual's overall fitness.

Flexibility

This is the ability of a joint or muscle to move through its full range of motion.

Static flexibility – involves holding part of the body still, at its full range of movement, such as holding a balance (gymnastics).

Dynamic flexibility – uses the full range of movement across a joint, where a fast action is used but not held, such as arching the back (high jump).

Sporting relevance

Flexibility is one of the main fitness components, important for success in many sports.

Key attribute	Part of the overall profile
Gymnastics	Racket sports
Diving	Team sports

Speed

This is the ability to move a distance in the shortest time.

Remember: speed is not just how fast someone can run, cycle or swim, but is dependent on acceleration (how quickly they can **accelerate from a stationary position**), maximal speed of movement, and **speed maintenance** (minimising deceleration).

Sporting relevance

Key attribute	Part of the overall profile
Track and field, sprints (100 m sprint/long jump)	Racket sports
Speed skating	Team sports

The athlete must accelerate from the starting block to maximum velocity in as short a time as possible.

Body composition

This is the amount of body fat and lean tissue the athlete has.

Body composition is exactly what the name states: what our bodies are composed of. In general, we are all made up of the same parts – muscle, bone, organs, tissue, and fat. However, fat in particular varies immensely from person to person. This is the primary focus of body composition: the percentage of stored fat in a body versus lean mass.

Sporting relevance

Key attribute		Part of the overall profile
Low body composition and low body fat	High body composition and high body fat	
Horse racing	Sumo wrestling	Racket sports
Gymnastics	Heavyweight boxing	Team sports

Now try this

Justify how the component 'speed' is only part of the overall profile required for a tennis player.

Skill-related fitness

This is important for performing the more technical aspects of many sports.

What is skill-related fitness?

Skill-, performance- or motor-related fitness involves skills that will enhance one's performance in athletic or sports events.

Skilled athletes typically excel in all areas.

Agility

This is the ability of the athlete to change direction quickly and accurately during sport while maintaining control of the movement.

Sporting relevance

Key attribute
Team sports – football
Racket sports – squash

Balance

This involves being able to maintain stability or equilibrium while stationary.

Static balance – where the athlete is stationary, such as a handstand in gymnastics.

Dynamic balance – where the athlete is moving, such as a gymnast performing a cartwheel.

Sporting relevance

Key attribute
Gymnastics
Surfing

Coordination

This is the ability to move two or more body parts under control, smoothly and efficiently, to perform a task.

Sporting relevance

Key attribute
Badminton, squash
Baseball, softball

Reaction time

This is the time taken for a sport performer to respond to a stimulus and initiate their response, such as the starting pistol (stimulus) and the sprint start (the movement) in sprint events.

Sporting relevance

Key attribute
Motorsports
Fencing

Power

This is the ability to generate and use muscular strength quickly over a short period of time, such as in accelerating, jumping and throwing implements.

Sporting relevance

Key attribute
Weightlifting
Boxing

Power = strength × speed

Now try this

Explain the importance of 'agility' for a footballer.

Aerobic training principles

Aerobic exercise strengthens the heart and lungs and trains the cardiovascular system to manage and deliver oxygen more quickly and efficiently throughout the body.

Frequency (F)

Ideally, two workouts a week will maintain fitness levels, but for nearly everyone three to five sessions a week would be better.

If fat loss is the goal, then six to seven low-impact workouts a week is optimal.

Intensity (I)

Heart rate is the primary measure of intensity in aerobic training. Before a training programme, a target heart rate zone should be determined.

These factors can be manipulated within aerobic training: time, distance, terrain, pace. There must be a balance between overloading the body (so it can adapt) but not so much that it causes overtraining.

Time (T)

How long someone performs aerobic exercise will depend on their goals, schedule, and physical condition.

In general, 20–60 minutes is acceptable.

If the goal is body fat loss and the athlete is appropriately conditioned, then longer is better: at least 30 minutes and ideally 40–60 minutes.

Type (T)

Selection of aerobic exercise depends on goals, physical condition, injury and illness history.

It is a good idea to 'cross train' – alternate between and among several appropriate exercises. This reduces the chances of overuse injuries, imposes more balanced conditioning and enhances enjoyment.

Maximum heart rate (MHR) and training zones

MHR is used to calculate how hard you should work your heart to develop either aerobic or anaerobic fitness. (MHR) can be calculated as follows: **220 – age = MHR.**

✓ **Warm-up or cool-down zone = 50** per cent of MHR (mainly for sedentary/unfit individuals new to training).

✓ **Activity recovery zone = 60** per cent of MHR (useful for aiding recovery, removing waste products; the next step for those new to training).

✓ **Fat burning zone = 60–70** per cent of MHR (required for fat burning management and for athletes training for long distances).

✓ **Aerobic fitness zone = 70–80** per cent of MHR (where you develop aerobic endurance; it is suitable for active/trained individuals).

✓ **Target heart rate = 60–75** per cent of MHR (this has the greatest benefit for cardiovascular health).

✓ **Peak performance zone = 80–90** per cent of MHR (highest zone of cardiovascular training, which is geared towards competitive sport and will help develop speed).

✓ **Anaerobic threshold = 90–100** per cent of MHR (this is the point where you can no longer meet your aerobic requirements, so the body uses your anaerobic systems. Training at this level is only suitable for advanced athletes).

Now try this

Your client, Julie, is 52 years old and she has decided to begin exercising.

(a) Calculate her maximum heart rate.

(b) What training zone would you recommend she works within?

(c) Work out her training heart rate.

Continuous and fartlek training

There are several different types of aerobic endurance training – each with a different, specific outcome and suitable for different events and sports.

Continuous training

This is also known as steady state training:

- training is completed at a steady pace over a long distance
- intensity should be moderate – aerobic training zone
- 20 minutes minimum up to several hours (e.g. marathon runners)

- suited to long distance athletes, such as runners or swimmers
- useful for beginners
- suited to athletes recovering from injury
- suited to specific populations – such as children, elderly people.

Advantages	Disadvantages
👍 Small amount of easy-to-use, accessible equipment, if any. 👍 Effective for aerobic fitness. 👍 Effective for losing weight.	👎 Can be boring. 👎 Doesn't improve anaerobic fitness – used in team games. 👎 Risk of injury. 👎 Not always sport-specific.

Continuous training can be **gym-based** using a treadmill, rower, cross trainer or bike, or **outdoors** at a suitable park/track.

Fartlek training

- Intensity is varied for the individual's specific needs, for instance a running session could include sprinting for 10 sec, fast walking for 20 sec, jogging for 1 min and repeating this.
- Intensity is varied by terrain or by pace.
- It can be more individual and sport-specific than continuous training.

- It uses both aerobic/anaerobic energy systems to improve aerobic endurance.
- It can involve changes in direction – which can closely mimic a sport.
- There are no rest periods.
- The athlete tends to have more control and is able to decrease intensity to rest.

Advantages	Disadvantages
👍 Less technical than other methods. 👍 Easy to use – adapt to level of fitness and sport. 👍 Athletes control their own pace. 👍 Boredom is reduced. 👍 Good for sports requiring a change in pace.	👎 Too easy to skip the hard sections. 👎 Can be difficult to see how hard an individual is training.

Fartlek training can be **gym-based** using a treadmill, rower, cross trainer or bike as long as the speed, resistance, and gradient can be changed regularly. It can also take place **outdoors** at a suitable park which has varying terrain, for instance sandy or hilly terrain.

Now try this

Which sports would utilise fartlek as a method of training?

Interval and circuit training

There are several different types of aerobic endurance training – each with a different, specific outcome and suitable for different events and sports.

Interval training

Interval training involves the following:

- improves both anaerobic and aerobic endurance
- varying intensity and work periods – for example, alternating periods of high-intensity exercise/effort with periods of low-intensity exercise/effort
- can be repeated, depending on fitness

- when designing the number of intervals, the intensity and duration of work and rest intervals, need to be considered
- allows for progression and overload by increasing work periods, increasing number of intervals, decreasing rest periods or increasing intensity of the rest period (for example a slow jog instead of a walk).

Advantages	Disadvantages
👍 Can mix aerobic / anaerobic, which replicates team games.	👎 Hard to keep going when you start to suffer fatigue.
👍 Can be easier to observe the athlete who is not trying.	👎 Can become boring.

Interval training can be **gym-based** using a treadmill, rower, cross trainer or bike as long as speed / resistance / gradient can be changed at the required intervals, or **outdoors** at a suitable park or track.

Circuit training

Circuit training involves the following:

- different exercises / stations
- set time to perform exercises – for instance, 1 minute per station
- rest periods in between stations
- can be designed for aerobic/muscular endurance or strength or a combination of all three

- stations should be structured to use different muscle groups
- to alter intensity: decrease the rest, increase the number of stations/circuits, increase the time spent at each station or increase the number of sessions per week.

Advantages	Disadvantages
👍 Less boring as it changes all the time.	👎 Takes a while to set up.
👍 Easily adapted for strength/endurance.	👎 Requires a lot of equipment.
👍 Easily adapted for different sports.	

Circuit training can be **gym-based** using a range of equipment, depending on space. Circuit training can use cardiovascular equipment, free weights, fixed resistance machines or body weight exercises. Circuit training can be performed **outdoors** at a suitable venue.

Now try this

(a) Which types of aerobic training would be most beneficial for a footballer player?

(b) Explain your answer to question (a).

Muscular strength training

Generally, individuals take part in weight training to increase their **strength**. Other reasons include improving muscle tone or muscle size.

Frequency (F)

Frequency is dependent on the individual and format of the programme.

- A programme that works every body part should be completed three to four days per week with rest days in between.
- A programme that focuses on just one or two body parts can be completed as frequently as six days per week.

Intensity (I)

Workload is the measure of intensity for strength training. Workload has three components: **1. weight, 2. number of repetitions (reps), 3. number of sets**.

- The number of sets depend on fitness levels/training experience/muscle areas.
- Rest: 2–4 min between sets. **Higher intensity = more rest. Lower intensity = less rest.**
- To prevent fatigue, large muscle groups should be worked first, then smaller.
- All muscle groups should be exercised to avoid an imbalance.
- Abdominals should be left until the end to avoid fatigue (as they act as a stabiliser whilst exercising other groups).

Time (T)

- Common consensus is no longer than 45–60 minutes.
- Intense sessions may last as little as 20–30 minutes.

Type (T)

Types include:

- resistance machines
- free weights
- medicine balls
- circuit training
- core stability training.

Pyramid sets

These are a highly effective technique, performing an exercise or two for a particular rep, then working your way down to one exercise, which is intended to suffer fatigue:

- upward/downward sequence in weight/reps/sets
- starting with a light weight allows the body to warm up
- involves an intense routine as the muscles become overloaded.

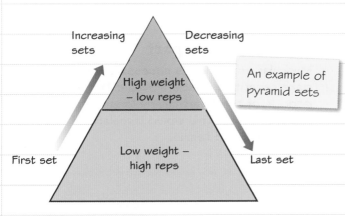

An example of pyramid sets

Equipment

Free weights

Advantages	Disadvantages
👍 Large muscle groups can be worked at once – saves time.	👎 Risk of injury.
👍 Can be used at home or at the gym.	👎 Heavy weights require a spotter.
👍 A full range of motion is used.	👎 More suited to advanced trainers.
👍 Functional to everyday and sport-specific movements.	👎 Requires good knowledge to use effectively.

Resistance machines

Advantages	Disadvantages
👍 Safer than free weights.	👎 Expensive – gym based.
👍 Used by beginners/injury rehabilitation.	👎 Focuses on one muscle group at a time.
👍 Guided range of movement.	👎 Not functional everyday movement.

Now try this

Would you recommend a beginner uses free weights or a resistance machines? Why?

Muscular endurance

Muscular endurance is the ability to repeat a series of muscle contractions without fatiguing.

Principles

We must train the muscles to overcome fatigue.

- Muscular endurance works on the principle of performing many repetitions against a given resistance for a prolonged period of time.
- It should come after muscular strength training.
- Its benefits are increased muscle tone and some hypertrophy. It creates an increase in size and number of mitochondria.

Frequency

- **Beginner:** 2–3 days per week.
- **Advanced:** 4–5 days per week.

Remember to incorporate rest to avoid over-training and injury.

Intensity (I)

Intensity varies:

- high reps and low loads: 15–30
- sets: 4–6
- light/medium resistance: 46–60 per cent of 1RM
- rest periods are short
- work largest muscle groups first then smaller groups
- ensure all muscle groups are worked to avoid an imbalance.

1RM = maximum amount of force that can be generated in one maximal contraction

Time (T)

The time involved per session varies:

- 30–60 min
- dependent on intensity of session
- 10–30 sec rest periods.

The work–rest ratio of 1:1 can be used here. This means spending the same amount of time resting as it took to complete the previous set.

Type (T)

Types include:

- free weights
- resistance machines
- circuits
- resistance bands/tubing.

Relevance to sport

Muscular endurance is necessary for people who make repetitive muscle movements for extended periods of time; particularly long distance runners and triathletes. This would translate into sports like football and tennis.

Now try this

Name a circuit training exercise used to develop muscular endurance in these three muscle groups:

(a) Legs

(b) Arms

(c) Stomach.

Core stability training

'Core stability' describes the ability to control the position and movement of the central portion of the body.

Principle

The core muscle groups include more than just the abdominal muscles. Other core muscles are the erector spinae, external obliques, internal obliques, rectus abdominis, transverse abdominis.

The **main function** of the core is to stabilise and provide support, to allow large amounts of power to be transferred to the extremities of the body.

Core stability plays an important role in postural balance and injury prevention.

Popular core exercises

These include:

- ✓ crunches
- ✓ the plank with variations (such as side plank/reverse plank)
- ✓ leg raises with variations
- ✓ superman or dead fish
- ✓ the bridge with variations.

Superman/dead fish pose

Yoga

Yoga focuses on core stability, strength, flexibility and breathing for physical and mental well-being. It:

- focuses on back / abdominals
- can use light weights / resistance bands
- can be used towards physical activity guidelines for adults – strengthening activities
- classes are usually 45 min to 1 hour.

Pilates

- Pilates focuses on core strength to improve general fitness and well-being.
- Exercises are done on a mat or using specialist equipment.
- Pilates has a system of pulleys, springs, handles and straps, thus providing resistance or support.
- It is appropriate for all ages, levels of ability and fitness, from beginners to elite athletes.

Gym-based exercise

- Exercise taken from both yoga / pilates can be conducted in a gym or at home.
- Gyms have various machines, which focus on core stability, such as back extension and abdominal crunch machines.

Equipment

Core stability exercises can now be enhanced by using additional core/balance equipment (such as kettle bells, medicine balls, stability discs, bosu or foam rollers), making them more challenging and fun.

Now try this

Identify **three** benefits of core stability training.

Flexibility training

By increasing the range of motion about a joint, performance may be enhanced and the risk of injury reduced. Various types of stretching improves flexibility.

Maintenance stretch

Good for: after the exercise session.

Why: to maintain general flexibility after exercising/return muscle back to its normal length.

How: 10–20 sec.

Type: usually static stretching.

A maintenance stretch is not meant to improve your flexibility and, as such, is not held for very long.

Developmental stretch

Good for: end of session or as a stand-alone flexibility session.

Why: to develop general flexibility/improve ROM.

How: initial 6–10 sec – progress to a deeper stretch, repeat until last stretch is 20–30 sec.

Type: usually static stretching.

Try to increase the depth of the stretch slowly over time.

Pre-activity stretch

Good for: pre-workout warm-up.

Why: muscles ready for exercise, to improve performance and reduce injury risk.

How: increase ROM over a series of 10–20 reps or for 8–10 sec.

Type: usually dynamic stretching and focusing on the muscles which are going to be exercised.

Pre-activity stretches provide an excellent opportunity to rehearse the movements an athlete is about to perform in their coming workout.

Static stretching

Static stretching is controlled and slow:

- **active** stretching involves the athlete moving the joint through its range of motion and holding it at the point of stretch themselves

- **passive** or **assisted** stretching involves a partner/object moving the joint to the point of tension in the muscle and holding it for the athlete, while they relax.

Dynamic stretching

Dynamic stretching replicates the kind of movements which are common in sports, and can be adapted to suit the sport and individual. It involves taking a muscle through its entire ROM; examples of these types of drills include high knees, lunges and heel flicks.

Proprioceptive neuromuscular facilitation (PNF)

PNF:

- is an advanced technique
- is effective for increasing flexibility
- alternates contraction and relaxation.

PNF usually involves a 10 sec push phase followed by a 10 sec relaxation phase, which is repeated several times.

Stretching equipment

Towel   Belt

Exercise ball   Stretch band

Equipment

Foam rollers   Exercise mat   Partner   Mat

Now try this

(a) Which type of stretching do you recommend for a netballer preparing for a match?

(b) Explain your answer to question (a).

Speed training: principles

Speed is one of the main fitness components, important for success in many sports.

Principles

- Good acceleration is vital.
- Acceleration from a standing position is required for team sports.
- Speed training should be sports- and position-specific.
- Speed training should follow a warm-up and any training within the session should be of a low intensity.
- Speed training should be conducted after rest or light training – to reduce injury/overtraining.

Training thresholds / % MHR

Sprinting is anaerobic, meaning athletes need to work in their anaerobic target zone while training between 80–100 per cent of their MHR.

Anaerobic threshold is the heart rate above which we gain anaerobic fitness. We cross our anaerobic threshold at 80–100 per cent of our MHR.

Peak speed should be towards 80–100 per cent – this would only make up a small percentage of the training time. Working anaerobically creates an oxygen debt so we can only keep going for a short time.

Recovery

This is:

- an essential part of speed training
- required to replenish energy stores/maintain correct technique and reduce injury risk
- recovery between speed sessions should be 72+ hours.

Factors influencing speed

These are:

- flexibility
- strength
- endurance
- technique.

FITT principle for speed

Frequency	2–3 sessions per week
Intensity	Intensity: 80–100%
	Peak speed: 90–100%
	Reps: 4–10
	Sets: 1–4
	Rest periods: 1–3 min between sets
Type	Acceleration training, hollow sprints, interval training, resistance drills
Time	5–20 sec time under tension

Work–rest ratio of 1:5 so 10 sec maximal sprint followed by a 50 sec rest period.

 Links Go to page 81 to revise the FITT principles.

Circuit training using FITT principle

Now try this

Why is recovery important for speed training?

75

Speed training: methods

Speed can be improved by completing one or a combination of the following training methods, best suited to the athlete's sport.

Hollow sprint

This method:

- replicates the pattern of a constant change of pace
- involves sprinting for a set distance, slowing down and accelerating for a set distance
- trains fast twitch fibres to accelerate over a short distance.

Example: Sprint 20 m, jog 5 m, sprint 15 m, jog 5 m, sprint 10 m and jog 5 m. Rest for 2 min then repeat for 1–4 sets.

Appropriate for team and individual sports, which require varying speed whilst competing.

Acceleration sprints

This is an aerobic training method.

- Speed is gradually increased: jog to stride to sprint.
- The progressive nature reduces the risk of injury.
- A slight incline can help with conditioning on the calf, thigh and hip muscles.

Example: 8 × 30 m hills at a 15 degree gradient. Walk back with a 2 min rest between each repetition.

Interval training

This method can improve anaerobic endurance and speed.

- Work intervals are short but intensity is near to, if not, maximal.
- Overload / progression can be incorporated by manipulating the rest periods.

Resistance drills

Using resistance when accelerating can develop speed over a short distance.

- This method makes muscles work harder.
- When resistance is removed, the athlete is ready to accelerate faster.
- Equipment includes resistance bands / parachute / sled / bungee ropes
- Resistance can be simply added by running up a hill or sand dunes, etc.

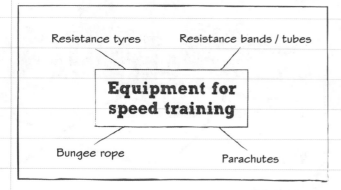

The importance of speed

The more efficiently you can run, the faster you can be.

- Therefore, technique is important with speed training.
- Good technique results in a more efficient use of energy.
- There are basically two phases to sprinting – the **acceleration phase** and the **top speed phase**.

Now try this

Is acceleration or top speed phase important for a footballer?

Agility and balance

There are several components of skill-related fitness; two important elements are agility and balance.

Agility

Agility is the ability of a sports performer to quickly and precisely move or change direction without losing balance or time. Agility is influenced by body balance, coordination, the position of the centre of gravity, running speed and skill.

This is an example of an agility drill for football.

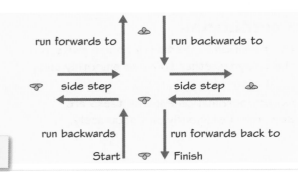

run forwards to | run backwards to

side step → | ← side step

run backwards | run forwards back to

Start | Finish

Improving agility

Agility can not only be improved by agility training drills, but also by improving the following elements: speed, balance, power and coordination. SAQ (speed, agility, quickness) training works over short distances (5 m) and with a zig-zag pattern between cones. It requires performers to perform the drills as quickly as possible, forcing changes of directions with correct technique.

Balance

Balance is the ability of the performer to maintain their centre of mass over a base of support.

Balance is used through all sport, but in certain sports its importance is greater.

Static balance

Static balance involves maintaining balance in a stationary position.

A gymnast uses static balance for a handstand on a balance beam.

Dynamic balance

Dynamic Balance involves maintaining balance in motion.

A gymnast uses dynamic balance for control within a cartwheel.

Improving balance

Improving balance is useful:

• to engage core muscles
• to prepare for a rapid change in direction.

Pilates and yoga are effective methods of training for balance.

Static training can involve one-legged balances. Once effective, this should progress to dynamic training.

Dynamic training can include a wobble cushion/balance board or exercise such as a squat on one leg.

The principles of progression can be incorporated here, from static to dynamic.

Now try this

(a) Choose a sport from the following and explain why agility is important: basketball, football or rugby.

(b) Give **one** reason why balance is important in a game of netball.

Coordination and reaction time

There are several components of skill-related fitness, two important elements are coordination and reaction time.

Coordination

Coordination is the ability to use parts of the body together to move smoothly and accurately.

Good coordination ensures tasks are performed efficiently and accurately.

Types of coordination

There are three types of coordination.

Hand–eye coordination, such as that needed for racquet sports.

Foot–eye coordination, for instance to keep a ball under control.

Hand-to-hand coordination, such as that needed in basketball to switch hands when dribbling the ball.

Improving coordination

Methods of improving coordination include:

1. **ball catching exercises**: throw a tennis ball against the wall, catching with one hand and then the other

2. **racquet drill**: bounce a ball on a racquet, palm facing up first, then alternate with palm facing up and palm facing down

3. **juggling drills** help with coordination and ball control.

Reaction time

Reaction time is the time taken for a sports performer to respond to a stimulus and the initiation of this response.

Reaction time is vital for sports that are timed and of short-duration, such as a 100 m sprint, a goalkeeper saving a penalty, a volleyball player reacting to a smash.

Poor reaction time in athletics can result in 'false starts', which mean an athlete could be warned or disqualified.

Reaction balls

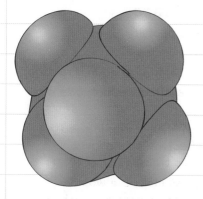

Reaction balls are usually six-sided and made from rubber, meaning they bounce irregularly and aid the development of hand-eye coordination and quick reaction time for players of any sport.

Other equipment that may be used for reaction-time training are: stopwatch, whistle, visual stimulus (flags, etc) and auditory stimuli (shouting, sounds, etc).

Improving reaction time

Two examples of reaction drills are:

1. **kneeling to sprint**: kneel on all fours; on a command given by the coach react quickly and sprint 10 m

2. **ball and drop reaction drill**: with a partner the ball should be held at shoulder height and out to one side of the body and then dropped. The athlete needs to react, accelerate and attempt to catch the ball before it bounces for a second time.

Now try this

Explain the importance of reaction time for a cricket batsman.

Power

Plyometric exercise is used in sport-specific training to enhance power and performance.

Plyometrics

Plyometrics is one of the most effective methods of improving power.

- ✓ It can benefit a range of athletes.
- ✓ Effectiveness relies on maximal effort and a high speed of movement for each repetition.
- ✓ Plyometrics is ideal for sports/activities that involve explosive actions, such as a slam dunk in basketball.
- ✓ It is most effective following maximal strength training.
- ✓ The skill/speed of performing a plyometric exercise is of importance.
- ✓ Athletes should stop before fatigue breaks down technique.

Frequency

- 2–3 sessions of plyometrics can be completed in a week.
- Alternatively, recovery time between sessions can be used to decide frequency and is recommended at 48–72 hours.
- Plyometric training should not follow a heavy weight training session, when muscles may still be sore. This can cause issues for athletes who may need to strength-train 3–4 times per week.

Intensity

- Plyometric exercises should be performed at 100 per cent effort.
- Skipping exercises are classed as low intensity, while reactive drop jumps from height are the most intense.
- Training should progress gradually from lower to higher-intensity drills.
- For lower-body exercises, reps are known also as ground contact.

Time

- Each set should last no longer then 6–8 seconds.
- Full recovery should occur between sets.

Plyometrics for different intensities:

- **low** – 10–30 reps, 10–15 sets, 2–3 min rest
- **sub-maximal** – 3–25 reps, 5–15 sets, 3–5 min rest
- **maximal** – 3–5 reps, 10–20 sets, 8–10 min rest.

Type

Exercises should try to mimic the movement patterns of the sport as closely as possible.

- **Lower-body plyometric exercises** such as squat jumps, bounding and box drills are suitable for sports such as basketball, track and field athletics, football or hockey.
- **Upper-body plyometric drills** such as medicine-ball throwing and catching, claps and push ups are suitable for sports such as basketball, volleyball, tennis or badminton.

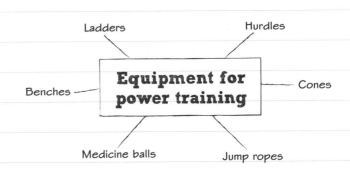

Ladders — Hurdles — Cones — Jump ropes — Medicine balls — Benches — **Equipment for power training**

Now try this

Provide **two** lower-body plyometrics exercises suitable for a basketball player.

Aims, objectives and SMARTER targets

To create the most effective training programme, an important question you need to ask first is: what is the individual's **specific fitness goal**?

Goal setting

Research has shown that goal setting has a positive effective on performance. The benefits are:

✓ giving the athlete an aim/focus/purpose

✓ increasing motivation

✓ increasing confidence level.

Aims

An aim is an intention or aspiration; what you hope to achieve.

The most common aims include:

- to build muscle/to increase strength
- to lose fat/to get 'toned'
- to gain/lose weight
- to improve performance
- to get in shape/to be healthier/to look better.

Objectives

An objective is a goal or a step on the way to meeting the aim and how you will achieve it.

Objectives use specific statements which define measurable outcomes (for example: what steps will you take to achieve the desired outcome?).

The SMARTER principle

When setting goals, the **SMARTER** principle should be applied to make your goals challenging, but attainable.

(S) Specific – make sure your goals are precise and stated in performance terms, such as, 'to complete my first 10 K race in the next three months'.

(M) Measurable – goals must be quantifiable to track progress, for instance measuring minute–mile pace with weekly tempo runs to ensure on target.

(A) Achievable – sometimes goals are set which are unattainable. Goals should be set high, but they must also be realistic, such as, 'I used to enjoy running, and I have time to train now'.

(R) Realistic – goals have to be within the performer's reach to increase confidence.

(T) Time phased – a set period must be stated in which the goal should be reached, to allow for progression to be monitored and evaluated, for instance three months..

(E) Exciting – the goal has to be motivational, for instance to improve the time of certain runs each week.

(R) Recorded – the progress has to be written down, to account for progress, such as distance and times.

Now try this

Why is it important that goals are agreed by the performer and the coach?

FITT principles

FITT principles are a set of rules that must be adhered to in order to benefit from any form of fitness programme.

Frequency / intensity / type / time

The four principles of fitness training are applicable to individuals exercising at:

- low to moderate training levels
- both aerobic and resistance training.

FITT is used to guide the development of unique and bespoke fitness plans that cater for an individual's specific needs.

Frequency

The frequency of exercise is a fine balance between providing just enough stress for the body to adapt to and allowing enough time for healing and adaptation to occur.

Frequency refers to the number of sessions per week.

Point to remember:

Beginners should start with approximately three sessions per week and build up to more.

Intensity

The principle of intensity defines the amount of effort/how hard you are working in your training programme. Like frequency, there must be a balance between finding enough intensity to overload the body (to adapt) but not so much that it causes overtraining.

Intensity refers to factors such as weight, distance and time .

Points to remember:

- HR (Heart Rate) is used to measure the intensity of aerobic exercise.
- Workload is used to define the intensity of resistance training.
- Only increase the intensity using one parameter; such as just weight and not reps, sets too.

Type

The principle of type dictates the exercise chosen to achieve the appropriate training response.

Examples are:

- **aerobic** – running, swimming, cycling (continuous, interval, fartlek)
- **strength** – resistance machines, free weight, circuits.

Points to remember:

- Consider the individual's sport / fitness levels.
- Consider personal preferences (likes / dislikes).
- Consider accessibility to equipment / facilities / finances.
- Ensure exercise is varied to avoid boredom and work a range of areas.

Time

The final component is time; how long you should be exercising for. For example:

- **Aerobic** – beginners should work for 20–30 min, working up to 45–60 min as fitness levels increase
- **Strength** – sessions should be no longer than 45–60 min; more intense sessions may last 20–30 min.

Beyond these times there is very little effect, and the individual runs the risk of overtraining and injury (with exception of a marathon runner).

Rest

An important extra principle is **rest**.

Over-exercising can prove to be detrimental to the training and the body.

The rule here should be: **the harder you train, the more recovery you should allow for.**

Now try this

You are required to design an aerobic training programme for a new client who would like to begin running.

Apply the principle of frequency to their training programme.

Principles of training

By using the principles of training as a framework, we can plan a personal training programme that uses scientific principles to improve performance, skill, game ability and physical fitness.

Specificity

Application of this principle means that training must be matched to the needs and demands of the sport you are training for.

It should be specific to the individual in terms of initial fitness levels, their strengths, weaknesses and goals.

Overload

Application of this principle means that fitness can only be improved by training above what you normally do (overloading). You need to work harder to allow the body to adapt and improve.

Overload is possible by varying the frequency, intensity or time of training.

Progression

This involves the gradual application of progression. This process needs to be gradual to avoid injury and overtraining.

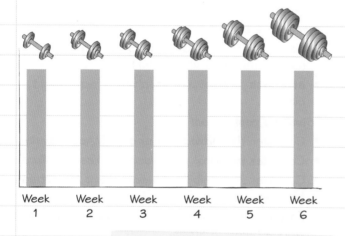

Week 1 Week 2 Week 3 Week 4 Week 5 Week 6

Start slowly and gradually increase.

Reversibility

This is also called 'detraining'. If you stop training, due to injury for example, any adaptations that have been developed as a result of training will deteriorate.

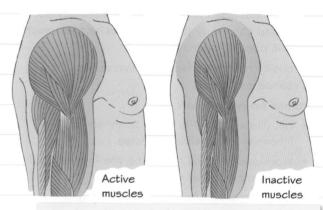

Active muscles   Inactive muscles

On the left is an image of a trained muscle, compared to an untrained muscle on the right.

Adaptation

This principle is the way the body 'programmes' the muscles to remember movement or skills. This ultimately encourages the body to adapt so the training becomes easier to perform.

Individual training needs

A successful training programme will meet individual needs, which are personal fitness needs based on age, gender, fitness level and the sport for which you are training.

Variation

Remember to vary training, to keep performers interested and to give the body a different challenge.

Rest and recuperation

Adequate time to rest and recover from training / competition is essential for both physiological and psychological reasons. Rest is physically necessary so that the muscles can repair, rebuild, and strengthen.

Now try this

One of the principles of training is reversibility.

What is meant by reversibility when training for an active healthy lifestyle?

Periodisation

Periodisation is simply known as a structured training cycle.

Ensuring optimum performance

Sports performers and their coaches must carefully plan their training programmes to ensure that optimum performance levels coincide with major events.

Periodisation ensures continued physiological and psychological changes; it prevents over-training, boredom and helps to achieve peak performance.

Main phases

A training year can be split into different phases, working back chronologically from a date where you wish to peak.

The **three** main phases are:

☑ off season (transition period)

☑ preseason (preparation period)

☑ in season (competition period).

Macrocycles

Macrocycles are 1-year to 4-year training cycles.

Examples:

- **Footballers** will work on a macrocycle from June–May, aiming to peak for weekly or bi-weekly matches.
- **Olympic athletes** will have a 4-year macrocycle, aiming to peak for the Olympic games.

Macrocycles are divided into a number of mesocycles.

Mesocycles

These are monthly training cycles.

- They are the main method of controlling the work-to-rest ratios (for example, 3:1 – work for three weeks followed by 1 active rest week).
- The technique uses a repetitive work-to-rest ratio, with a 4-week mesocycle and a ratio of 3:1, this could then be repeated but the intensity increased.

Each mesocycle is divided into a number of microcycles.

Microcycles

These are weekly or individually planned training sessions.

- Specific adaptations are the focal point and should demonstrate the FITT principles.
- Microcycles typically last for a week or can range between 5 and 10 days.

Individual training sessions

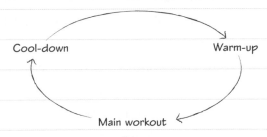

Three basic components should be included in any training session.

Now try this

Give **three** reasons for the importance of periodisation within training.

About your Unit 2 assessment

Familarise yourself with the assessment structure of Unit 2, Part A and Part B.

Part A

Part A will be issued two weeks before your supervised assessment (Part B). It will be in the form of a **scenario** based on an individual who requires guidance on:

- training
- lifestyle
- nutrition.

For Part A, you will conduct **independent research** and produce up to **four sides of A4 notes**, which can then be used in the supervised assessment (Part B).

Research for Part A is expected to be carried out over approximately **eight hours**.

Your teachers/tutors cannot give any support to the notes and you must complete the work independently.

Part B

Part B will be **assessed externally** using a written assessment in the format of a **task booklet**. The assessment will take place under **supervised conditions** and will last **two hours**. Within Part B you will be issued with additional stimulus information building on the scenario information in Part A. You are allowed to use your prepared notes produced in Part A, but these **do not** need to be submitted at the end of the assessment.

Preparation

It may be useful to conduct secondary research in the following areas and prepare notes on these before your assessment:

- ✓ lifestyle factors and their effect on health and well-being
- ✓ recommendations to promote health and well-being
- ✓ screening processes for training programming, including health monitoring test
- ✓ nutritional programming requirements
- ✓ training methods for different components of fitness
- ✓ appropriate training activities to meet the needs of a selected individual
- ✓ principles of fitness training.

Now try this

Identify the key elements to the assessment of Unit 2.

Part A: Reading the brief

Understanding the key points of the task brief and information is imperative before you begin to complete Part A.

Hints for reading the brief

✓ Read and take time to consider the instructions carefully.

✓ Read through the set task brief and make a list of the areas suggested to research.

✓ Read through the set task information as a whole.

✓ Read through the information again and highlight or underline key words/points about the client. You can make notes as you read through.

Key points of information

When reading the set task information consider the key pieces of information provided.

Consider Mrs Smith's **age**, particularly in terms of the type of exercise and possibly her fitness levels.

Is Mrs Smith's **lunch break** a long enough opportunity to include some element of physical activity?

What are Mrs Smith's **current physical activity** levels and what type of **exercise/sport** does she currently do? What exercise is she looking to start? Think about government recommendations.

Mrs Smith is 40-years-old, she works 9–5 pm as a Receptionist at a dentist's surgery. She has the car on most days and drives the 1 mile to work. When she doesn't have the car, her husband drops her off. She takes 45 min for her lunch each day. The staff at the dentist surgery are signed up to take part in a charity triathlon, but Mrs Smith hasn't run or cycled for a number of years, however she is a regular swimmer and is a member of the local swimming club. The triathlon is 6 weeks away. Mrs Smith attends her gym and takes part in a fitness assessment and will afterwards receive a personal training programme. She has previously completed a PAR-Q and has indicated that she has no medical conditions and is fit to take part in activity.

Think about her **occupation**, her working hours and how active/inactive will she be at work.

Consider her **transport** to and from work. Could exercise be incorporated here?

Consider her **goal**. The training programme will focus towards this.

Consider Mrs Smith's **medical conditions**.

Now try this

Use the above scenario based on Mrs Smith.

Practise preparing introductory notes addressing the key pieces of information identified in the scenario above.

Part A: Conducting research

You may benefit from conducting secondary research and preparing notes on the following key areas. Below are examples of content checklists alongside some exemplar notes.

Key areas 1 and 2: lifestyle factors and modification techniques

- Exercise / physical activity ☑
- Balanced diet ☐
- Smoking ☐
- Alcohol ☐
- Stress ☐
- Sleep ☐
- Barriers to change ☐
- Strategies – physical activity ☐
- Smoking-cessation strategies ☐
- Strategies – reduce alcohol consumption ☐
- Stress management techniques ☐
- Blood pressure ☐
- Resting heart rate ☐
- Body mass index ☐
- Waist-to-hip ratio ☐

> Use a checklist to ensure that you cover the relevant areas.

Links Go to pages 44–57.

> Exemplar learner notes for exercise and physical activity.

Sample notes extract

Mrs Smith is a regular swimmer participating twice a week for 45 minutes per session. In comparison to government recommendations this is positive:

Mrs Smith is used to moderate exercise.

Negative:

She needs to expand her training to cover the other elements of a triathlon – running and cycling.

She would also benefit from spreading her activity across more days of the week,

she should also incorporate some low weight training, in order to achieve the government recommendation of 75 minutes per week.

> Only include relevant information; e.g. government recommendations for below 19, and above 64 years are irrelevant for Mrs Smith.

> Government recommendations for adults (19–64 years).

Key area 3: nutrition

- Nutritional terminology ☐
- A balanced diet ☐
- Nutritional strategies ☐

Think about: Analysing the client's current diet and strategies that could be incorporated to improve it. Remember to consider their future physical plans here.

Links Go to pages 58–64.

Key area 4: training methods

- **Physical fitness components:** aerobic endurance, muscular strength, muscular endurance, core stability, flexibility, speed ☐
- **Skill-related fitness components:** agility, balance, coordination, reaction time, power ☐
- Training methods for each of the above ☐

Which are the most appropriate training methods for the individual, goal or sport?

Key area 5: principles of fitness training

- Aims/objectives ☐
- Goals ☐
- FITT principles ☑
- Additional principles ☐

Think about: Consider these aspects when designing your training programme.

> Exemplar learner notes on frequency from FITT principle.

Sample notes extract

Frequency – Mrs Smith is not a beginner; already swims twice a week. Increase sessions to 3/4 then to 5 in latter part of programme. At least two rest days each week. Include variety to train for different elements of a triathlon.

Now try this

You know that that Mrs Smith is preparing to complete a triathlon.

Consider the rest of the FITT principles and prepare suitable notes (intensity, type, time).

Questions on interpreting lifestyle

Lifestyle questionnaire

At the start of your Part B task booklet you will be given additional information about the individual in your set task information. This will be in the form of a completed lifestyle questionnaire, containing the following information:

- ✓ personal details
- ✓ current activity levels
- ✓ nutritional status
- ✓ lifestyle
- ✓ health monitoring tests
- ✓ physical activity/ sporting goals.

🔗 Links Go to pages 44–48.

🔗 Links Go to pages 54–57.

🔗 Links Go to pages 65–79.

Answering Part B

- ✓ Note the number of marks available for each question.
- ✓ For longer questions, you will be required to include a number of explanations.
- ✓ Plan and structure your answers – consider what you need to cover.
- ✓ Support you answer with research, such as normative data for blood pressure.
- ✓ Read your answer through once completed.

You will need to effectively interpret the lifestyle factors and screening form for the selected individual using both your research and the information from the lifestyle questionnaire.

Worked example

1 Interpret the lifestyle factors and screening information for the selected individual. **12 marks**

Sample response extract

Health monitoring tests for Mrs Smith: Blood pressure (BP) – 135/82 mm Hg; Body Mass Index (BMI) – 25; Waist-to-hip ratio (WHR) – 0.81; Resting heart rate (RHR) – 78 bpm.

Mrs Smith's blood pressure is pre-high this could be negative for her health. Her BMI and waist-to-hip ratio highlight she is not at an ideal weight. This could also affect her health. Her resting heart rate is 78 bpm, which is average.

An interpretation of health monitoring test results is attempted but this is generic; lacking relevance to the individual.

🔗 Links Go to pages 54–57.

Improved response extract

Mrs Smith is 40 years old. Her BMI and waist-to-hip ratio compared to normative data suggests she is slightly overweight. Her BMI of 25 is just inside the overweight category, with 24 being classed as normal. Her waist to hip ratio is 0.81, putting her at moderate risk, with 0.80 being low risk. As Mrs Smith is only slightly overweight, it would mean small changes to her physical activity and diet to see changes to her BMI and WHR results. The negative impact of being overweight for Mrs Smith could include her developing diabetes, high blood pressure and many other health problems. Mrs Smith's BP is both classed as pre-high and normal, her systolic is 135, which is classified as pre-high BP. Her diastolic reading is 82, which is classified as normal. As one figure is above the normal level, Mrs Smith BP is classified as pre-high BP. This can impact negatively on Mrs Smith's health causing an increase risk to the heart, which puts her at greater risk of a stroke and a heart attack. Mrs Smith's resting heart rate of 78 bpm is classified as average for her age. This is positive for her health, and with increased training over time her resting heart rate should decrease further.

A detailed analytical approach, leading to an interpretation of health monitoring test results; interpretation is specifically relevant to the individual.

Now try this

Consider Mrs Smith's monitoring results as a whole.

Suggest **two** ways in which Mrs Smith could work towards changing her health monitoring results.

Questions on lifestyle modification

For your assessment you will need to provide lifestyle modification techniques for your client to promote their health and well-being.

Lifestyle factors

☑ Smoking   ☑ Stress   ☑ Diet

☑ Alcohol   ☑ Sleep   ☑ Physical activity

> Remember the lifestyle factors you should be suggesting modification to.
> For each lifestyle factor, there are several techniques. Choose the most suitable for the client.

Worked example

2 Provide lifestyle modification techniques (alcohol).   12 marks

> No relevance to the individual.

Sample response extract

She should drink less alcohol as she is above the government limit.

This could be achieved by not drinking every day or by drinking smaller measures or drinks with less alcohol. They could avoid rounds and stay in more often.

It might be a good idea for them to try counselling or yoga to help reduce alcohol intake. Some of these strategies are free and are provided by the NHS.

> General techniques, assumption that the individual drinks alcohol only while out. Mrs Smith indicated on her screening form that she drinks 15 units of alcohol per week.

> General and limited relevance to the individual's requirements.

Improved response extract

Mrs Smith consumes 15 units of alcohol per week, which exceeds the government recommendations. Reducing alcohol consumption is therefore a priority to Mrs Smith's health and also to support her training for the forthcoming triathlon.

There are strategies that Mrs Smith could try before seeking external help. Firstly, suggestions will be made for drinking while at home. Mrs Smith should try to drink alcohol alongside food and avoid leaving the bottle on the table, which can cause temptation and over-consumption. Drinking at home may mean that Mrs Smith pours her own measures and drinks the bottle just because it is open. To avoid this, Mrs Smith could use a smaller glass or even measure her drinks or simply keep track of her intake. Whilst at home, Mrs Smith may drink at the same time of day, so breaking habits and finding distractions could also be an easy solution. Exercise particularly can break habits and, as Mrs Smith is preparing to complete a triathlon, planning her training at times when she would normally drink could be a simple strategy.

As she will be increasing training, she may decide that training does not combine well with drinking alcohol and this could be a good opportunity to reduce or even stop drinking. Mrs Smith may drink while out, so strategies to try are to set herself a limit of alcoholic drinks, alternating with non-alcoholic drinks where possible. She should avoid rounds, which will allow her to drink at her own pace rather than to keep up with others.

As Mrs Smith doesn't excessively exceed the government recommendations, I think she should try the self-help strategies first, which entail minor lifestyle changes, before seeking external support from self-help groups, counselling, etc.

> Relevance to client throughout answer.

> Specific relevance to individual's lifestyle and requirements.

> Alternative strategies suggested.

> Justification is relevant to the individual's lifestyle.

> 🔗 **Links** Go to page 51 to revisit this topic.

Now try this

Mrs Smith has indicated that she doesn't hit the prescribed hours of sleep per night.

Suggest **three** suitable strategies to improve this.

Questions on nutrition

For your assessment you will need to provide nutritional guidance for your client.

Nutritional guidance

- ✓ The Eat Well Plate and choices of food
- ✓ Timing and number of meals
- ✓ Fluid intake (including affeine/alcohol)
- ✓ Portion sizes, organisation and preparation
- ✓ Training needs

Mrs Smith's diet

Breakfast	Toast
Lunch	Cheese and tomato sandwich (white), crisps
Dinner	Pasta with garlic bread
Snacks	Cake, cheese and biscuits, chocolate bar, cheesecake
Fluid intake	Coffee (2 cups), tea (1 cup), water (1.5 litres), white wine (2 small glasses)

Worked example

3 Provide nutritional guidance.

8 marks

Sample response extract

Mrs Smith needs to alter her diet; she should eat more carbohydrates, more fruit, vegetables and fish. She needs to cut down on saturated fat, sugary foods and salt.

She should drink more water each day and drink less caffeine and alcohol. She needs to make sure she eats more food now that she is starting to train for her triathlon.

Generic guidance.

Limited relevance to individual's dietary requirements.

Improved response extract

Mrs Smith eats breakfast, providing a good start to her day. However, this could be swapped with a healthier choice, such as cereal, which would increase her intake of calcium and carbohydrates required to supply energy. Or maybe a smoothie, which would contain both fruit and vegetables, supporting Mrs Smith towards achieving her five-a-day.

Specific relevance to the individual's requirements.

For lunch, she could modify her sandwich choices by using brown bread and swapping the cheese and tuna and cheese and tomato sandwiches to a tuna salad sandwich, containing less saturated fat and more protein. Her crisps could be swapped for a healthier alternative such as rice cakes, cashew or pistachio nuts. Another item of fruit or dairy such as yoghurt could be added to her lunch menu to offer a balance of food groups. Her tea includes a base of carbohydrates, which is recommended as well as meat and vegetables. The garlic bread could be removed as it might be high in fat. Her takeaway option should be avoided, with her opting to cook something homemade such as chicken stir fry, which would offer both protein and vegetables. Mrs Smith's snack choices could be adapted with items such as the slice of cake, cheese and biscuits, chocolate bar and cheesecake, all high in saturated fat and sugar, being removed and replaced with fruit. Mrs Smith should plan her meals ahead and use the Eat Well Plate as a basis for ensuring all food groups are included.

Mrs Smith's hydration is an area which needs addressing. Although she does not exceed the recommendations for caffeine intake, she would benefit from swapping caffeine drinks for more water. She is currently below the recommendation of 2–2.5 litres per day. A way to encourage herself to drink more water is to have a bottle on her desk while at work. Mrs Smith would also benefit from reducing her alcohol intake, as alcohol contains empty calories which are of no use to the body.

A justification of hydration guidance.

When training for her triathlon, she will need to ensure she eats the right amount of calories for her increased activity. She should consider supplementing her diet with more complex carbohydrates, which will offer her 'slow release energy'. This could be in the form of wholegrain pasta, rice and nuts, etc.

Specific relevance to individual's requirements.

Now try this

Explain **one** nutritional strategy you would recommend Mrs Smith to use prior to her triathlon.

Questions on training methods

For your assessment you will need to propose relevant training methods for your client.

Training methods

✓ **Physical related components** – aerobic, strength, muscular endurance, flexibility, speed, body composition.

✓ **Skill-related fitness** – agility, balance, coordination, reaction time, power.

> For each component there are several types of training methods. Consider the most suitable for the individual and their goal.

Worked example

4 Training methods.   8 marks

Sample response extract

Mrs Smith needs to do more cardiovascular training, such as running, cycling, rowing. She could do continuous, interval and fartlek training.

She does swim but she doesn't participate in any other training. She should start off with training at a low intensity and build this up over the weeks of training.

> Mrs Smith indicated on her screening that she swims twice a week.

> Methods are generic, with limited relevance to the individual's training requirements.

 Links Go to pages 68–70 to revisit cardiovascular training methods.

Improved response extract

Mrs Smith's training aims are towards completion of a triathlon. She already swims twice a week, but needs to incorporate both cycling and running into her weekly routine.

I suggest including two extra training sessions per week, which will focus on aerobic training to improve her cardiovascular fitness. Alongside this training, muscular endurance and strength training could also be incorporated to support the requirements of a triathlon and due to the fact she currently does no strength training during the week.

Training should be heavily based on running, cycling and swimming to specifically prepare for the triathlon. Her initial cardiovascular training would be low to moderate intensity (that of a beginner) as Mrs Smith hasn't completed these types of exercise for a number of years, so to begin with she would be working within the activity recovery zone of 60 per cent of her MHR, eventually working towards 70–80 per cent MHR to improve her cardiovascular fitness.

Continuous training is suitable for a beginner like Mrs Smith, but it is also an effective method for her training goal of a triathlon. However, a variety of training methods will be included to avoid repetition and boredom.

Although she already swims, her swimming training would be adapted to imitate this event within the triathlon, given the fact that a certain number of lengths have to be completed as fast as possible.

> Specific relevance to the individual's training requirements.

> Specific relevance to the individual's training needs.

> Justification for proposed training methods, relevant to the individual's training needs.

> Justification.

> Specific relevance to her training aim and individual needs.

 Links Go to pages 68–79 to revisit training methods for the various components of fitness.

Now try this

Explain **one** additional aerobic training method suitable for Mrs Smith to use within her training.

Questions on training programmes

You will need to design a six-week training programme for the selected individual.

Training programme
✓ **Principles of training** – specificity, progression, overload, reversibility, adaptation, variation, individual training needs, rest and recuperation.
✓ **FITT principles** – frequency, intensity, time and type.

> Some of the areas you should consider when designing a six-week training programme.

Worked example

5 Design key stages of a six-week training programme – week 1. **6 marks**

> Limited understanding of the principles of training, such as overload, individual training needs, intensity, and time within each activity.

Sample response extract

	Mon	Tues	Wed	Thurs	Fri	Sat	Sun
Physical activity	Rest day	30 min swim moderate pace	Rest day	30 min bike moderate pace	30 min swim	Rest day	30 min run moderate pace

> Generic detail, limited relevance to the fitness requirements of the individual, such as pace for a beginner, training thresholds.

> Certain requirements are omitted, such as intensity, the breakdown of the activity, warm-up, cool-downs.

> Specific activities for a triathlon are included.

Improved response extract

> Variation, overload, specificity, rest, individuality, FITT principles included.

	Mon	Tues	Wed	Thurs	Fri	Sat	Sun
Physical activity	Rest day	30 min swim – 50 m easy warm-up; 16 × 25 m – 30 sec rest / interval; 50 m cool-down	Rest day	30 min bike / run 20 min bike; 10 min run as 2 × 4 min jog; 1 min walk after each jog (conversational pace / 60%–70% MHR = 108 bpm–126 bpm)	30 min swim as easy warm-up; 25 m, 50 m, 75 m, 100 m, 75 m, 50 m, 25 m all on 30 sec rest / interval; cool-down	Rest day	45 min bike / run 30 min outdoor ride 15 min run as 3 × 4 min easy jog; 1 min walk after each jog (conversational pace / 60%–70% MHR = 108 bpm–126 bpm)

🔗 **Links** Go to pages 80–83 to revisit this topic.

> Combines all three events within a triathlon.

> Intensity is suitable for a beginner and training thresholds are specific to the individual.

Now try this

Look specifically at Tuesday's swimming session in Week 1 (improved response). Suggest **two** ways progression could be incorporated.

Answering 'justify' questions

You will need to justify the six-week training programme for the selected individual.

Justification

✓ The individual's **aim/level of fitness/current exercise routine / sport**.

✓ **Principles of training** – specificity, progression, overload, reversibility, adaptation, variation, individual training needs, rest and recuperation.

✓ **FITT principles** – frequency, intensity, time and type.

> Some of the areas you should consider when justifying your six-week training programme.

Worked example

6 Provide justification for the training programme that has been produced for the selected individual (Week 1).

`14 marks`

Sample response extract

> Limited understanding of the principles of training.

The programme has four training days and three rest days; this would change over the six weeks.

It incorporates swimming, cycling and running as Mrs Smith requires these sports for a triathlon and so she doesn't get bored. She will need to work at a moderate pace in her activities and build this up over the six weeks.

> Limited relevance to the training requirements of the individual.

Her training sessions are all 30 min, which is acceptable for aerobic training.

Improved response extract

The training programme focuses on developing aerobic fitness in preparation for her triathlon. Specifically running, cycling and swimming are included. Overload is included by ensuring that she is working above what her body is normally used to. Although she swims, her current exercise regime includes no running or cycling.

> The words highlighted demonstrate a thorough understanding of the principles of training applied to the training programme.

With this in mind, the intensity of running and cycling is a suitable level for her as a beginner. A variation of training methods is incorporated with no training day identical, allowing for greater progress and to ensure Mrs Smith does not become bored. Rest and recuperation is incorporated; week one includes three rest days, and as the weeks progress this will decrease to two days to allow for more training. The programme is individual for Mrs Smith, considering her aim, level of fitness and current exercise regime. The frequency of the sessions is four per week; two of her current sessions, with two additional. Together these ensure she achieves the government targets for physical activity but also trains towards the triathlon.

> Specifically relevant to the requirements of the individual.

Intensity is set to a challenging yet realistic level for Mrs Smith with recovery periods in all sessions in the form of a 30 sec rest period or the pace altering to walking. Heart rate thresholds are utilised to ensure she is working her aerobic system at the right level for a beginner, but also for adaptation and progress to be made. During future training, factors will be manipulated to ensure progression, such as rest periods, heart rate, pace, etc. The time of all sessions is 30 min plus, this is an optimal time to develop aerobic fitness whilst also considering her fitness levels.

Now try this

On the previous page you suggested **two** ways progression could be incorporated. Justify the suggestions made.

Answers

Unit 1 Anatomy and Physiology

1. The skeleton

(a) Kyphosis is when the back is hunched due to an abnormally large curve of the thoracic vertebrae.

(b) Kyphosis could have a negative impact in games activities because in games it is an advantage to know the positioning of opponents and team mates. This is easier with neutral spine alignment because of the position of the head.

2. Bone growth

To return to rugby Karl, will need his broken arm to heal, this is possible through the action of the bone cells osteoclasts and osteoblasts. Osteoclasts break down the damaged bone, reabsorbing this bone tissue. This would reduce the bone density, reducing the strength of the bone, but the osteoblasts maintain bone mass by increasing the bone matrix, meaning Karl's arm repairs ready to return to the rugby field.

3. Functions of the skeleton

The cranium protects the brain from injury – for example: concussion when heading a football, as it provides a hard shell around the organ preventing direct impact from the ball onto the brain. The ribs protect the heart and lungs in contact sports like rugby by encasing these vital organs so that when tackled, the heart and lungs remain unaffected underneath the rib cage.

4. Bone types

Long bones act as levers so that you can bring the racket through a greater range of motion at pace, allowing you to put more force on the shuttle, this means you are more likely to get the shuttle to the back of the court, or play a more effective smash to win the point.

5. Joint classification

The joints of the upper skeleton: shoulder, elbow, wrist, cervical and thoracic vertebrae.

The joints of the lower skeleton: hip, knee, ankle, lumbar, sacrum and coccyx vertebrae.

The elbow allows the player to straighten the arm for the ball toss, movement at the shoulder allows the player to rotate the arm to hit the ball with force, the wrist allows them to grip the racket and the vertebrae allow slight movement so the player can arch their back to get a more powerful serve.

6. Joints use in sport

(a) Each joint between the vertebrae allows a small amount of movement – small movement along the length of the spine allows the high jumper to arch their back to achieve the shape necessary to clear the bar.

(b) Pivot joint at neck – in a long distance race when turning the head to check where the other runners are. Ball and socket joint at the hip – allowing the leg to follow through after kicking a ball. Hinge joint at the knee – when bending the leg at the knee as part of a running action. Hinge joint at the elbow – bending the arm to complete a biceps curl. Condyloid joint at the wrist – when taking the hand back to serve in volleyball. Gliding joint at the foot – sideways stepping action just before releasing a javelin. Saddle joint at the thumb – gripping the parallel bars in a gymnastic routine. Ball and socket joint at the shoulder – allows the upper arms to move together to complete the butterfly action in swimming.

7. Joint structure

The bursa cushion impacts within the joint. They are there to protect the joint. Therefore, when the player is thrown, there is less chance of damage to the joint so the performer can continue to train and compete.

8. Anatomical position

Carrying the javelin during run-up (flexion) and then as it is released the arm extends at the elbow. A batsman playing a forward defensive in cricket needs flexion at the elbow to get the bat over the ball. In a golf swing the arms go from extension to flexion (at the top of the swing) back to extension as the ball is struck.

9. Abduction and adduction

(a) Adduction is moving towards the anatomical position but abduction is moving away from it.

(b) Horizontal abduction means taking the limb away from the body but in a horizontal plane, for example a discus thrower horizontally abducts the arm at the shoulder as the arm stays at shoulder height as it moves away from the midline.

10. Other ranges of movement

By checking the elbow position during the technique because in horizontal flexion the elbow points to the sides rather than to the floor.

11. Responses and adaptations

It is important to warm up so that the skeletal system can respond to this exercise rather than waiting until the game starts. For example, in hockey you need to bend a lot at the waist. If you can't, your techniques such as dribbling or stopping the ball will not be as good, but by warming up the ligaments become more pliable to increase the movement possible at the joint to allow you to get into the low position you need to be effective right at the start of the game.

12. Additional factors

(a) It will mean the performer has restricted movement, making it very difficult for the performer to move in the way they need to for their activity.

(b) By increased calcium levels in the bone.

(c) As their bones are still developing and this increase in heavy weight could reduce long-term bone growth.

13. Muscle types

The cardiac muscle of the heart contracts forcing blood through the heart to the lungs to gain oxygen or through the body to the working muscles. This means that blood is delivered to the muscles carrying the oxygen needed for sustained exercise. Without skeletal muscle we couldn't move so we wouldn't be able to play sport, for example use our legs to run or our arms to propel a wheelchair to complete a sprint event. Without smooth muscle we wouldn't be able to move food into the digestive system and therefore unable to get the nutrients required for energy to participate in physical activity.

14. The muscular system

The supinators would allow the player to cup their hands around the ball to catch it.

15. Antagonistic muscle pairs

Anterior and posterior deltoid; hamstrings and quadriceps; tibialis anterior and gastrocnemius, hip flexors and gluteals, biceps and triceps.

16. Muscle contraction

Concentric muscle contractions are needed when we move, for example in the hamstrings when running they contract and shorten to allow flexion at the knee. Isometric muscle contractions occur in static balances, for example when holding a headstand, the muscle does not lengthen or shorten. Eccentric muscle contractions occur when the muscle lengthens under tension, for example during the downward phase of a press-up when the triceps eccentrically contract to control the descent.

17. Fibre types

They can recruit the different fibre types depending on what they need to do within the race, for example, for most of the race they will use type I for steady state running over a prolonged period of time, maintaining their pace to keep with the pack. However, if they need to sprint, they would recruit type IIx as these produce a more powerful contraction and therefore would help them accelerate past opponents. Without the range they could either only go at one pace, or wouldn't be able to last the length of the race – either way, performance would be worse.

18. Responses

Both Jermaine and Jill would experience increased muscle temperature and their muscles would become more pliable, and both would have increased blood flow to the muscles. Jermaine's muscles would begin to accumulate lactic acid, whereas Jill's would be more likely to suffer microtears.

19. Aerobic adaptations

If Becky carries out regular aerobic training she will increase the number and size of the mitochondria in her muscles. This means she will be able to produce more energy aerobically giving her the energy she needs to continue to play well for longer, reducing the chance that she will be substituted.

20. Anaerobic adaptations

If Igor is using interval training to increase his speed his training sessions will be anaerobic, therefore he will increase his ability to store ATP-PC which will give him a greater energy supply so he will be able to sprint for longer, therefore he will improve his 200 m time.

21. Additional factors

You can try to reduce cramp by stretching before the race and making sure you drink enough fluids during the race to maintain hydration and electrolyte balance.

22. The respiratory system

Air enters the body via the nasal cavity. From here it passes through the pharynx, larynx and trachea on its way to the lungs. It travels through the bronchi and then bronchioles before ending up in the alveoli.

23. Respiratory function

(a) The blood in the capillary is returning from the muscles so oxygen has been used up, but the alveolus contains air that has just been breathed in so has a greater concentration of oxygen.

(b) Steeper gradient during exercise as more oxygen would be extracted from the blood.

24. Lung volumes

Tidal volume will increase from normal breathing to forced breathing so that a greater volume of air moves into and out of the lungs per breath. This lung volume can increase until vital capacity is reached.

25. Control of breathing

Chemoreceptors detect changes in carbon dioxide levels as more is produced due to exercise, which causes a drop in blood pH. The medulla oblongata responds to this information by speeding up the messages sent to the respiratory muscles to contract and relax to increase breathing rate.

26. Responses and adaptations

Increase in breathing rate and tidal volume.

27. Additional factors

So that their bodies become used to the reduced partial pressure of oxygen at altitude and begin to compensate for this by increasing their red blood cell count so that sufficient oxygen can still be transported to the muscles.

28. The cardiovascular system

Deoxygenated blood passes from the vena cava to the right atrium. From here it travels through the tricuspid valve into the right ventricle. It then passes through the semi-lunar valves into the pulmonary artery to travel to the lungs. It returns from the lungs and passes through the pulmonary vein to the left atrium. From here it travels through the bicuspid valve into the left ventricle where it is then pushed out of the heart, passing through the semi-lunar valves into the aorta and then on to the rest of the body.

29. Blood and blood vessels

Arterioles.

30. Functions of the cardiovascular system

Transport of oxygen / carbon dioxide / lactate. Maintaining body temperature at 37° C. Fighting infection. Clotting wounds.

31. Cardiac cycle

The parasympathetic nervous system sends messages to the SAN to reduce heart rate, for example during recovery from exercise. The sympathetic nervous system sends messages to the SAN to increase heart rate, for example during exercise.

32. Responses

To increase the amount of oxygen supplied to the working muscles so they can get the required energy for exercise and to remove the additional waste materials generated through increased energy production.

33. Adaptations

We don't need resting heart rate to be as high as a greater volume of blood can be ejected from the heart per beat due to the increased stroke volume. Therefore, we don't need the heart to beat so many times to eject the same volume of blood per minute. As cardiac output = heart rate × stroke volume, if we increase stroke volume we reduce resting heart rate so that cardiac output remains the same.

34. Additional factors

So that people are aware of any medical issues you may have or any family history of illness that might affect how much physical exertion you should do.

35. The role of ATP

(a) ADP is adenosine di-phosphate.

(b) Muscle ATP lasts for 2–3 seconds.

(c) The ATP-PC system, the lactic acid system and the aerobic system.

36. The ATP-PC system

High jump competition, where there are several minutes between jumps.

37. The lactate system

(a) Lactate.
(b) The lactate increases the acidity of the blood which decreases the efficiency of energy production. Therefore, the muscles become fatigued as they are not getting the required energy.

38. The aerobic system

Because this energy system produces far more molecules of ATP from one molecule of glucose than the anaerobic systems, therefore the body has sufficient energy to maintain activity over a long period of time. However, due to the number of processes required to produce energy through this system, it cannot be produced quickly. This makes it unsuitable for intense activity where energy needs to be supplied rapidly to allow rapid muscle contraction.

39. Adaptations

(a) Increased use of fats and stores of glycogen, increased mitochondria.
(b) This means more fuel sources available for breakdown in energy production, and more places in the muscles where this can occur, therefore better energy production, i.e. the performer can work for longer.

40. Additional factors

To reduce the likelihood of having a hypoglycaemic attack.

41. About your Unit 1 assessment

ATP is made up of one molecule of adenosine and three molecules of phosphate. The end phosphate breaks from the chain releasing energy for muscle contraction.

42. Command words

There is an increase in blood flow to the skeletal muscle as during exercise the muscles need more oxygen for energy production and to remove the additional oxygen generated. To increase blood flow to the muscles the arterioles supplying them vasodilate to increase the space available for blood flow. At the same time the arterioles supplying inactive areas such those leading to the digestive system vasoconstrict, making it harder for the same quantity of blood to pass through so that more blood can be funnelled through the arterioles supplying the muscles.

43. Long-answer questions

Appropriate levels of exercise would be good as they help to lower blood pressure. The cardiovascular system adapts to the regular exercise, causing a drop in resting blood pressure, and also decreasing the risk of heart-related ill health. Several factors contribute to a drop in resting blood pressure. When we train, the heart undergoes cardiac hypertrophy, this means the heart muscle increases in size and becomes stronger. It can contract with more force and therefore doesn't have to work as hard. There is also an increase in nitric oxide released in the blood vessels. This stimulates the blood vessel to vasodilate, which means the space for the blood to flow through increases, reducing blood pressure. There is also an increase in plasma volume so there is less risk of the blood becoming too viscose, increasing blood pressure. These are all positive outcomes and would help Becker. However, as Becker already has high blood pressure he needs to make sure that the exercise he does is gradual, especially after such a long absence from sport. A potential problem is that a short-term response to exercise is an increase in blood pressure, therefore if Becker's blood pressure is already high a further increase could, in extreme cases cause stroke or cardiac arrest as the blood is unable to flow properly through the blood vessels. This is why it is recommended that people see their GP before exercising for a long time to make sure it is safe for them to do so, and the level of intensity they should work at. Overall, provided Becker is sensible and starts off at a low intensity, gradually increasing over time, exercise should help reduce his blood pressure as the body adapts.

Unit 2 Fitness Training and Programming for Health, Sport and Well-being

44. Exercise and physical activity

(a) Comparing Jack to government recommendations, he does not hit the target of 30 min of moderate exercise five times per week. He exceeds the vigorous activity of 75 min as he completes 120 min; however this is condensed into two days. He does not complete any strength training at all.
(b) Jack would benefit from more moderate exercise on at least 3 more days a week. He could spread out his vigorous activity over the other days of the week and it is recommended he participates in strength training twice a week.

45. A balanced diet

(a) *Answer to include any two of the following:*
   • pack items to eat on the move – fruit, breakfast bars, yoghurts
   • prepare smoothies
   • prepare breakfast the night before
   • wake up 10 min earlier
   • have breakfast items at work.
(b) All beverages can contribute to your fluid requirement (e.g. coffee and tea). The issues with these are they contain caffeine and sugar; therefore these are only appropriate in moderation.

46. Negative effects of smoking

Answer to include any three of the following:
   • several different cancers
   • heart-related conditions
   • lung-related conditions
   • respiratory conditions
   • infertility
   • smell – clothes, hair, etc.
   • yellow teeth / bad breath
   • passive smoking.

47. Negative effects of alcohol

Each evening Sam consumes approx 6.9 units × 4 nights per week = 27.6 units per week. Sam is therefore drinking nearly double the government recommendations. He spaces his alcohol intake over a 4-day period, but drinks above the levels recommended.

48. Stress and sleep

(a) Paul is 2 hours below the NHS recommendations for sleep.
(b) Lack of sleep can cause further stress as (*answer to include any two of the following*):
   • it can effect concentration, the ability to make decisions, memory, judgement and mood, which could affect home and work life
   • lack of sleep can make daily routines even more difficult
   • you may feel tired and unmotivated
   • you may skip exercise if tired
   • it may make you drink / smoke more.

49. Barriers to change

Answer to include any two of the following:
Two strategies you could suggest to your client who 'find exercise boring' are to encourage them to vary their routine and try new

exercise training methods. Exercising with a partner can reduce boredom; perhaps make it competitive between you both.

50. Smoking cessation strategies

Answer to include any two of the following:
Encourage the client to partake in more exercise, to break up routin; to maintain weight. Alongside this, the client needs to consume a balanced diet and snack on healthy snacks when cravings occur.

51. Reducing alcohol consumption

Answer to include any two of the following:
Two strategies for a client who drinks more than the recommended units per week while out are: only take out a set amount of money for alcohol and then you have to stop. Avoid drinking in rounds with friends and then you can limit your drinks and take breaks, alternating alcoholic drinks and soft drinks.

52. Managing stress

Answer to include any two of the following:
- releases feel good endorphins
- distracts the individual from the stressor
- can be free
- can improve sleep patterns which in turn reduces stress
- makes you feel better about yourself
- boosts energy levels
- improves mood.

53. Screening processes

(a) *Answer to include any two of the following:*
- gain information from client
- can be used as a basis to ask additional questions
- can detect those at risk of health issues.

(b) *Answer to include any two of the following:*
- individuals may lie / exaggerate the truth
- enough information isn't always given
- forms could be rushed.

54. Blood pressure

(a) Systolic reading – 138 – pre-high blood pressure, Diastolic reading – 86 –pre-high blood pressure.

(b) The areas on a screening form which need to be analysed in order to make recommendations for reducing blood pressure are: *Answer to include any four of the following:*
- age – the risk of developing high blood pressure increases as you get older
- a family history of high blood pressure
- certain origin – especially African or Caribbean origin
- diet/nutrition – particularly a high intake of salt/caffeine
- a lack of exercise
- being overweight or obese
- smoking
- drinking large amounts of alcohol
- high stress levels.

55. Resting heart rate (RHR)

(a) Chris's resting heart rate is categorised as poor for his age range.

(b) The areas on a screening form which need to be analysed in order to make recommendations for reducing resting heart rate are: *Answer to include any four of the following:*
- diet/nutrition
- a lack of exercise
- being overweight or obese
- smoking
- drinking large amounts of alcohol
- high stress levels.

56. Body mass index (BMI)

(a) $\dfrac{85}{1.75} = \dfrac{48.5714286}{1.75} = 27.76 = 28$

(b) *Answer to include any two of the following:*
- body fat content
- muscle mass
- bone density
- overall body composition
- where a person carries his / her body fat
- racial and gender differences.

57. Waist-to-hip ratio

(a) 39/37 = 1.05.

(b) It indicates that Rob is categorised as high risk.

(c) Recommendations based on WHR alone are (*answer to include any two of the following*):
- a combination of increased exercise / physical activity alongside a balanced diet
- to reduce alcohol intake.

58. Nutritional terminology

(a) Compared to RIs, this provided 30 per cent of an adult's daily intake for saturated fat. This product is therefore high in saturated fat.

(b) As this item has 'red' coding, this product needs to be eaten less often and in small amounts.

59. Energy balance

(a) Weight gain occurs when, over a period of time, we consume more energy than we actually expend (eating more than exercising).

(a) Weight loss occurs when, over a period of time, we don't eat enough for the amount of energy being expended (exercising more than eating).

60. Macronutrients

Often endurance athletes significantly increase their consumption of carbohydrates in order to maintain levels of muscle glycogen, delay fatigue, replenish vital stores and ultimately improve performance. For endurance athletes carbohydrates are the vital energy source, typically making up 55–65 per cent of an endurance athlete's total calorie intake. This leads to a significantly reduced proportion of fat intake (<20 per cent) The proportion of fat intake is reduced as it does not provide an endurance athlete with the necessary nutrients to support training and competition.

61. Vitamins A, B and C

Answer to include any two of the following:
(a) Vitamin A – sweet potato and carrots
(b) Vitamin B – eggs, and vegetables
(c) Vitamin C – strawberries, broccoli

62. Vitamin D, calcium and iron

It is not necessary for an athlete to take extra supplements provided the athlete is consuming a balanced diet and is meeting their energy requirements.

63. Hydration and dehydration

It is vital for maximum benefit and optimal performance that athletes strategically test and practise their fluid replacement strategies during training to ensure they are appropriately hydrated and to avoid impairing their performance within a competition. Athletes will need to plan when they will rehydrate to avoid an imbalance – this is best suited to take place within a practice setting.

64. Nutritional strategies

Both athletes require protein within their diet, either for a small proportion of energy or to assist in the repair, growth and recovery process after exercise. Power athletes who want to gain muscle size and function require more protein in the early stages of intense weight training.

65. Aerobic strength and muscular endurance

Triathlons are endurance based, therefore muscular endurance allows the body to perform the constant repetitions required by the muscles for the activities, e.g. swimming, cycling and running.

66. Flexibility, speed and body composition

Due to the nature of the sport of tennis, all the physical- and skill-related components of fitness are required. 'Speed' is an important aspect but possibly cannot be singled out as the most important. The sport of tennis requires other components, including aerobic endurance, ability, etc.

67. Skill-related fitness

In football, an agile player can respond quicker to an opposing player, closing down or jockeying. An agile player has the ability to explosively brake, change direction and accelerate again. Regardless of your position, you need to be able to accelerate and change direction quickly. In football, the ability to accelerate, decelerate and perform rapid movements in all directions is more important than simply running fast.

68. Aerobic training principles

(a) $220 - 52 = 168$ bpm
(b) As a beginner it is recommended that Julie works within the warm-up or cool-down zone = 50 per cent of MHR to the activity recovery zone = 60 per cent of MHR.
(c) Julie's training heart rate is 84–100 bpm.

69. Continuous and fartlek training

The advantage of fartlek training is that it can be adapted to various sports, individual or team events. This type of training is designed to mimic the demands of the sport so can be planned for any sport.

70. Interval and circuit training

(a) Fartlek and interval training are both suitable training methods for a footballer.
(b) Both methods work on the work/rest ratio which mimic the sport of football.

71. Muscular strength training

Answer to include any one of the following:
Beginners are more suitable to resistance machines rather than free weights because resistance machines are easier to learn and use. Free weights require skill to learn the proper technique and can put an individual at risk of injury if not used correctly.

72. Muscular endurance

Answer to include any one of the following:
(a) squat, lunge
(b) press up, bicep curl
(c) sit up, plank

73. Core stability training

Answers to include any three of the following:
- increases stability
- offers more support
- increases power to extremities of the body
- appropriate for all ages, levels of ability and fitness
- improves general fitness
- improves flexibility
- improves strength.

74. Flexibility training

(a) Dynamic stretching in a pre-workout warm-up is recommended for a netballer preparing for a match.
(b) It prepares the muscles for exercise and can reduce injury risk, and focuses on the muscles which are going to be used.

75. Speed training: principles

Answer to include any one of the following:
The amount of rest in training changes the benefits gained and the physiological systems targeted. In general, the higher intensity an activity is, the faster it is, and the more recovery is needed. Therefore, longer recovery periods are recommended for high-intensity training.

76. Speed training: methods

Acceleration is the most important for a footballer as the quickest player over the pitch will be the one who can accelerate the most rapidly.

77. Agility and balance

(a) *Answer to include any one of the following:*
Agility helps performance in activities that require you to change direction quickly whilst keeping balance, strength, speed and body control.
(b) Balance is important in a game of netball for many reasons
Answer to include any one of the following:
- you need it to keep a stable posture to ensure that you do not do footwork)
- when you are defending, it is good because it is closely linked to agility and you must be balanced before you change direction at speed
- when shooting to keep still
- if you end up on one foot and have to pass.

78. Coordination and reaction time

Answer to include any one of the following:
In cricket the ball is travelling so fast, requiring the batsman to respond to stimulus and initiate a response within seconds. They need to evaluate the delivery of the ball and respond, selecting the most appropriate shot. Hand–eye coordination is vital for any role in cricket such as batting. It requires the cricketer to watch and react to the ball so that tasks can be performed efficiently and accurately.

79. Power

Answer to include any two of the following:
- arm swing squat
- jump squat
- bounding
- weighted jump squat
- box jump
- depth jump
- single-leg box jump
- single-leg bounding
- single-leg depth jump
- alternating leg jumps.

80. Aims, objectives and SMARTER targets

Answer to include any one of the following:
- so there is shared responsibility with planning and setting goals
- so both parties are aware of the goals
- so the coach can motivate accordingly.

81. FITT principles

Answer to include any one of the following:

As they are a beginner new to running it is important that they start off with no more than three sessions per week. It is important to gradually build up the frequency as their fitness levels increase – the frequency of their new training programme needs to be manageable or they will struggle to adhere to it and drop out.

82. Principles of training

Reversibility is the principle of training which describes the loss of fitness, training benefits and adaptation when training has stopped. This break in training might be due to injury/illness or a holiday (e.g. footballers who are on holiday in the summer months).

83. Periodisation

Answer to include any three of the following:

- for appropriate planning/programming
- to work towards important dates/events
- to reduce the risk of injury
- to ensure progression
- to promote recovery
- for variation within training
- to ensure there is a correct balance of training
- for the fun element.

84. About your Unit 2 assessment

Student response exemplar notes:

Part A

- two weeks before assessment set task brief
- four sides of independent research in 8 hours
- no support from staff.

Part B

- external assessment
- task booklet set by Pearson
- controlled conditions
- lasting 2 hours
- supplementary material
- use notes from Part A.

85. Part A: Reading the brief

Exemplar notes:

1 Age – 40 yrs, active swimmer, not hitting government recommendations for exercise/physical activity.
2 Occupation – desk/inactive job, works 9–5, exercise would need to fit around these hours.
3 Transport – travels by car or gets a lift. She could walk/run/cycle to and from work at a reasonable distance.
4 Lunch – 45 min – she could manage a short walk, probably not too long/intense, given that she has to return to work.
5 Current exercise – swimmer – twice a week, not achieving government targets.
6 Goal – triathlon in 6 weeks – three elements –running, swimming and cycling.
7 Medical – no issues.

86. Part A: Conducting research

The remaining three FITT principles are:

- Intensity:
- These factors can be manipulated within aerobic training: time, distance, terrain, pace.
- It is a good idea to 'cross train' – alternate between and among several appropriate exercises.
- Training thresholds:
  - activity recovery zone = 60 per cent of MHR (the next step for those new to training
  - fat burning zone = 60–70 per cent of MHR (for athletes training for long distances).

- Type:
  - aerobic training required for a triathlon
  - swimming, cycling, running
  - aerobic training methods – continuous, interval, fartlek, some strength training.
- Time:
  - sessions to last between 20 and 60 min – start off lower and increase as her fitness increases.

87. Questions on interpreting lifestyle

Suggestions to improve Mrs Smith's health monitoring results would be (*answer to include any two of the following answers*):

- changes to her diet
- increase her physical activity
- reduce alcohol intake
- reduce caffeine intake.

88. Questions on lifestyle modification

Suitable strategies to improve sleep could be:
answer to include any three of the following:

- a regular bedtime routine
- avoid drinking coffee and tea
- take exercise during the day/avoid exercise two hours before bed
- ensure sleeping environment is comfortable
- avoid a heavy meal two hours before bed
- avoid using alcohol to help you sleep
- keep a to-do list beside the bed
- have a warm bath
- listen to relaxing music
- try breathing techniques.

89. Questions on nutrition

Nutritional strategies which could be used are: (*answer to include any correct strategy and one of the following:*

- Ergogenic aids –gels/bars:
  - help replenish carbohydrates/glycogen/calories
  - deliver a quick supply of energy to muscles on the go
  - light and easily digestible
  - designed for consuming on the go.
- Protein supplements, usually before or after exercise:
  - increase muscle size
  - increase muscle strength
  - reduce muscle soreness post-training
  - accelerate gains in aerobic strength
  - accelerate gains in anaerobic strength
  - result in greater fat loss when dieting
  - result in fat loss even when not dieting
  - reduce hunger.
- Carbohydrate loading:
  - eat a high-carbohydrate 'training diet' while scaling back your activity level
  - most beneficial for endurance athletes
  - completed the week prior to high-endurance activity.
- Sport drinks:
  - isotonic – quickly replace lost and boost carbs
  - used by athletes.

90. Questions on training methods

Other suitable training methods are:

- Fartlek:
  - intensity varied by terrain/pace
  - no rest periods
  - mimic a sport.
- Interval
  - work/rest/work.
- Circuit:
  - combine aerobic and strength
  - different exercises/stations
  - rest periods/changeovers.

91. Questions on training programmes

Progression could be incorporated into Tuesday's swimming by (*answer to include any two of the following*):

- increasing duration of session
- increasing lengths
- reducing rest periods
- increasing pace.

92. Answering 'justify' questions

Not all these aspects would be manipulated at once (*answer to include any two of the following*):

- increasing duration of session – for example from 30 to 35 min so that more exercise is completed – slight change to overload the body and to ensure progression towards a triathlon
- increasing lengths – for example from $16 \times 25\,m$ to $18 \times 25\,m$, etc so more exercise is completed, slight change to overload the body and to ensure progression towards a triathlon
- reducing rest periods – they could reduce to 20 sec, even if duration or lengths change this could stay the same
- increasing pace – lengths could be timed to assess pace and this could then be improved on.